Here is a life-giving tonic for today's church. From beginning to end – right through to his enthralling appendices – John Stott has given us gold on every page. *The Living Church* deserves to be read, discussed – yes, and re-preached – by pastors and Christian workers, ordained and lay, at every level and across every Christian denomination going. It ought to become required reading, not only in campuses and seminaries worldwide, but – because of its sheer readability – in everyday homes and fellowships where God's people are to be found.
Richard Bewes, former rector, All Souls Church, Langham Place

For many Christians, church has become a meeting to attend rather than an essential identity. So it is great to have John Stott looking at the Christian community with his typical clarity. He makes the Scriptures speak with immediacy to our contemporary challenges. With so many people considering the future shape of the church, this is a timely book, offering, as it does, biblical parameters for the discussion within a trinitarian framework.
Tim Chester, church planter with The Crowded House

Here is another book by John Stott which can be regarded as the standard treatment of the topic addressed. The advantage of Stott's books is that they not only present the biblical teaching on the topic comprehensively but that they also take the contemporary scene into account. As always this book of Stott is inspiring and nourishing reading.

There is a lot of confusion among Christians today about how we should 'do church' in this postmodern society. As we grapple with this we must always start with the biblical basics of church life and then apply those to the culture. This book presents these essential features that should be seen in churches in every age, and it does so in a way that makes it easy to apply to our contemporary culture.

Ajith Fernando, National Director, Youth for Christ

This is a gem of a book. Here is the heartbeat of a godly and faithful minister of Christ, whose influence for good has been, and continues to be, incalculable. Full of distilled biblical wisdom, refreshing candour and honesty, penetrating discernment and plans for practical action, it speaks with clarity and power to the confused and often demoralized contemporary church, with a message that is pure gold. This is a book which every committed Christian needs to read!

David Jackman, President, the Proclamation Trust

Exceptional clarity, profound concern and strong counsel are hallmarks of this last in a great series of written works by John Stott, for which Christians everywhere are thankful to God, and to him.

Dick Lucas, Rector Emeritus, St Helen's Church, Bishopsgate

In a time of questioning and turmoil around what a real church should look like in the twenty-first century, *The Living Church* is a beautifully written, inspiring and thoughtful book. The reader is given a vision for a church whose

roots are deeply biblical and whose touch reaches a dying world. As I read, I laughed, cried and ended up on my knees before God. I wholeheartedly commend this book.
Amy Orr-Ewing, Director of Training,
RZIM Zacharias Trust

John Stott has become a grandfather of evangelicalism to the entire world. His name is known everywhere and the influence of his writings and his preaching has been felt by thousands upon thousands. This, his latest book, will add to that influence. His insightful and clear way of expressing profound biblical truths will help the church to regain its sense of identity. How wonderful to have his resource made available to us at this stage of the church's history. This book will be an enormous help and encouragement to all who read it and in particular to the new generation of preachers and Bible teachers.
Frank Retief, Presiding Bishop,
Church of England in South Africa

This is vintage Stott, with all his familiar qualities: faithful, rigorous biblical exposition; crystal clarity; challenging contemporary applications with plenty of punch; great wisdom – not least in holding to the balances of Scripture without blunting its edges.
Vaughan Roberts, Rector of St Ebbe's Church, Oxford

John Stott

ivp

The
Living
Church

Convictions of a lifelong pastor

INTER-VARSITY PRESS
Norton Street, Nottingham NG7 3HR, England
Email: ivp@ivpbooks.com
Website: www.ivpbooks.com

First published 2007

British Library Cataloguing in Publication Data
A catalogue record for this book is available from the British Library.

ISBN 978–1–84474–183–0

Set in Adobe Garamond
Typeset in Great Britain by CRB Associates, Reepham, Norfolk
Printed and bound by Creative Print and Design (Wales), Ebbw Vale

*Inter-Varsity Press publishes Christian books that are true to the Bible and that
communicate the gospel, develop discipleship and strengthen the church for its
mission in the world.*

*Inter-Varsity Press is closely linked with the Universities and CollegesChristian
Fellowship, a student movement connecting Christian Unions in universities and
colleges throughout Great Britain, and a member movement of the International
Fellowship of Evangelical Students. Website: www.uccf.org.uk*

Dedicated
to
Michael Baughen
Richard Bewes
and
Hugh Palmer
who
followed me as successive
Rectors of All Souls Church
Langham Place London
and who stood and stand in the
same evangelical tradition

ACKNOWLEDGMENTS

I thank Michael Baughen, Richard Bewes and Hugh Palmer, who all followed me as Rectors of All Souls, for their friendship and leadership, and for allowing me to dedicate this book to them. I also thank Frances Whitehead, my longstanding and long-suffering secretary, who has served me under all three Rectors and who has typed this manuscript. And thirdly I thank Tyler Wigg Stevenson, my current Study Assistant, who has read widely on 'church', has made many suggestions, and has helped me to write the Preface.

ABBREVIATIONS

NAB   The New American Bible (NT 1970; OT 1969)
NEB   The New English Bible (NT 1961; OT 1970)
NJB   The New Jerusalem Bible (1985)
NIV   New International Version (1973, 1978, 1984)
REB   The Revised English Bible (1989)
RSV   The Revised Standard Version of the Bible
      (NT 1946; second edition 1971; OT 1958)
RV   Holy Bible, Revised Version (1885)

CONTENTS

PREFACE:
'EMERGING CHURCHES'

'If the current evangelical renewal in the Church of England is to have a lasting impact, then there must be more explicit attention given to the doctrine of the church.'

Thus spoke Robert Runcie, Archbishop of Canterbury, during his visit to the third National Evangelical Anglican Congress (NEAC), named a Celebration, at Caister-on-Sea in Norfolk in 1987.

Robert Runcie's words divided us. Some nodded their assent, fearful that his stricture was correct. But others protested vigorously, having 'turned away from the stubborn individualism for which we used to be notorious'.[1]

What is clear is that during recent years there has been an extraordinary proliferation of books about the church. I am thinking, for example, of *The Church on the Other Side* (1998), *The McDonaldization of the Church* (2000), *Changing World, Changing Church* (2001), *Church Next* (2001), *The Provocative Church* (2002), *Liquid Church* (2002), *The Prevailing Church* (2002), *Mission-Shaped Church* (2004), *The Emerging Church* (2004), *The Church Invisible* (2004), *God's New Community* (2005), *The Responsive Church* (2005) and *Emerging Churches* (2006). And this is only a sample from today's exploding library of popular ecclesiology. One could continue the list with reference to seeker churches, purpose-driven churches and others.

What has precipitated this avalanche of books is the sense that the church is increasingly out of tune with contemporary culture, and that unless it comes to terms with change, it faces extinction. Of course it will not die, for Jesus promised that even the powers of death will not overcome it. Yet alarming statistics warn us of the current crisis, and the language of 'seismic' change enforces the situation.

It is not that the church's calling is to ape the world, for it is called rather to develop a Christian counter-culture. At the same time, we must listen to the voices of the world in order to be able to respond to them sensitively, though without compromise. For example, in the Church of England, the Archbishops of Canterbury and York have sponsored the development of 'fresh expressions of the church',[2] in part to proclaim the gospel relevantly in an increasingly postmodern population that views the church as a relic.

> *The church's calling is to develop a Christian counter-culture.*

THE POSTMODERN WORLD

Keen-eyed social analysts are still trying to summarize what is involved in the cultural shift from the modernism of the Enlightenment to the arrival of postmodernism. The prefix 'post' in the word does not simply mean 'after'. It rather hints at a protest against the Enlightenment years and the collapse of the intellectual and social edifices of modernism. Indeed, postmodernism is essentially parasitic on modernism, as a remora clings to a shark.

One has only to list a set of antitheses to recognize that both modernism and postmodernism are extremely varied phenomena. In general, modernism proclaims the autonomy of the human reason, especially in the cold objectivity of science, whereas postmodernism prefers the warmth of subjective experience. Modernism is committed to the quest for truth, believing that certainty is attainable; postmodernism is committed to pluralism, affirming the equal validity of all ideologies, and tolerance as the supreme virtue. Modernism declares the inevitability of social progress; postmodernism pricks the bubble of utopian dreams. Modernism exalts self-centred individualism; but postmodernism seeks the togetherness of community. Modernism is supremely self-confident, often guilty of that arrogant ambition which the ancient Greeks called *hubris*, whereas postmodernism is humble enough to question everything, for it lacks confidence in anything.

Some characteristics of postmodernism, in its critique of modernism, are to be applauded, and offer new opportunities for the gospel, whereas others are to be rejected. One needs discernment to determine which is which.

What then are the marks of a church in a postmodern culture, that is, of an 'emerging church'? Most agree that what is evolving is as yet more a conversation than a movement, and are modest enough not to claim too much, since the situation is continuing to develop.

At the time of my writing, the most thorough analysis of

such churches is *Emerging Churches* by Professors Eddie Gibbs and Ryan Bolger of Fuller Theological Seminary, sub-titled 'creating Christian community in postmodern cultures' (SPCK, 2006). It is the fruit of five years' research, during which the authors listened to more than fifty leaders of innovative churches, and allowed them to tell their own stories.

From this comprehensive survey Eddie Gibbs and Ryan Bolger identified nine 'patterns' or 'practices' which kept appearing, three of which were 'core' practices common to the other six. Each is then given a chapter in the rest of the book.

> *Following Jesus, rejecting dualism and developing community should characterize every church.*

The first is 'identifying with the life (or way) of Jesus', namely both his example and his teaching as verbalized in the Sermon on the Mount.

The second is 'transforming secular space' that is, rejecting the sacred-secular divide promoted by modernism.

The third is 'living as community', indeed as a kingdom or family community.[3]

To be sure, these three 'core' practices do not appear very new, since following Jesus, rejecting dualism and developing community should characterize every church. Nevertheless, what should be the case often differs from what actually is. And so, because many church structures actually inhibit these core practices, emerging churches are rediscovering them and giving them a fresh emphasis.

It seems to me that traditional and 'emerging' churches need to listen attentively to one another, with a view to learning from one another. The former must recognize that much of what we recognize as traditional today was itself once revolutionary and even 'emerging', and therefore be open to today's creative thinking. The latter should be wary of loving newness for newness' sake. We both could afford to be less suspicious, less dismissive of one another, and more respectful and open. For, as Archbishop Rowan Williams has written, 'there are many ways in which the reality of "church" can exist'.[4] Nevertheless, it has certain essential marks which will always characterize an authentic and living church.

I have often said that we need more 'R.C.' churches, standing now not for Roman Catholic but for Radical Conservative churches – 'conservative' in the sense that they conserve what Scripture plainly requires, but 'radical' in relation to that combination of tradition and convention which we call 'culture'. Scripture is unchangeable; culture is not.

The purpose of this book is to bring together a number of characteristics of what I will call an authentic or living church, whether it calls itself 'emerging' or not. I hope to show that these characteristics, being clearly biblical, must in some way be preserved.[5]

Chapter 1

ESSENTIALS:
GOD'S VISION FOR
HIS CHURCH

As we begin to consider the essential marks of a living church, I am making three assumptions.

First, I am assuming that we are all committed to the church. We are not only Christian people; we are also church people. We are not only committed to Christ, we are also committed to the body of Christ. At least I hope so. I trust that none of my readers is that grotesque anomaly, an unchurched Christian. The New Testament knows nothing of such a person. For the church lies at the very centre of the eternal purpose of God. It is not a divine afterthought. It is not an accident of history. On the contrary, the church is God's new community. For his purpose, conceived in a past eternity, being worked out in history, and to be perfected in a future eternity, is not just to save isolated individuals and so perpetuate our loneliness, but rather to build his church, that is, to call out of the world a people for his own glory. Indeed, Christ died for us, not only 'to redeem us from all wickedness', but also 'to purify for himself a people that are his very own, eager to do what is good' (Titus 2:14). So then, the reason why we are committed to the church is that God is so committed. True, we may be dissatisfied, even disillusioned, with some aspects of the institutional church. But still we are committed to Christ and his church.

The church lies at the very centre of the eternal purpose of God.

Secondly, we are all committed to the mission of the church. We believe that the church has a double identity. On the one hand we are called out of the world to belong to God, and on the other we are sent back into the world to witness and to serve. Moreover, the mission of the church is modelled on the mission of Christ. He himself said so. 'As the Father has sent me, I am sending you' (John 20:21). His mission meant for him the incarnation. He did not stay in the safe immunity of his heaven. Instead, he emptied himself of his glory and humbled himself to serve. He actually entered our world. He took our nature, lived our life, and died our death. He could not have identified with us more closely than he did. It was total identification, though without any loss of identity, for he became one of us without ceasing to be himself. He became human without ceasing to be God.

And now he calls us to enter other people's worlds, as he entered ours. All authentic mission is incarnational mission. We are called to enter other people's social and cultural reality: into their thought-world, struggling to understand their misunderstandings of the gospel, and into the pain of their alienation, weeping with those who weep. And all this without compromising our Christian beliefs, values and standards.

Thirdly, we are all committed to the reform and renewal of the church. In many parts of the world, especially in significant regions of Africa, Asia and Latin America, the church is growing rapidly, although often the growth is in size rather than in depth, for there is much superficiality of discipleship everywhere. Nevertheless it is growing. In other parts of the world, however, especially in the West, if

What is God's vision for his church?

I may generalize, the church is not growing. Its development is stunted. Its waters are stagnant. Its breath is stale. It is in a state not of renewal but of decay. We long to see it continually being reformed and renewed by the word and the Spirit of God.

Having considered our threefold common commitment (to the church, to its mission and to its renewal), we are ready to ask a basic question: what is God's vision for his church? What are the distinguishing marks of a living church? To answer these questions we have to go back to the beginning and take a fresh look at the first Spirit-filled church in Jerusalem on the Day of Pentecost. Mind you, as we do so, it is essential that we are realistic. For we have a tendency to idealize or romanticize the early church. We look at it through tinted spectacles. We speak of it in whispers, as if it had no blemishes. Then we miss the rivalries, the hypocrisies, the immoralities and the heresies which troubled the first-century church as they trouble the church today.

The early church had been radically stirred by the Holy Spirit.

Nevertheless, one thing is certain. The early church, in spite of all its excesses and failures, had been radically stirred by the Holy Spirit. So what did that early church look like? What evidence did it give of the presence and power of the Holy Spirit? If we can answer these questions, noting carefully the essentials which Luke mentions in Acts 2, we will be able to discern the marks of a living church today. Luke focuses on four marks:

They devoted themselves to the apostles' teaching and to the fellowship, to the breaking of bread and to prayer. Everyone was filled with awe, and many wonders and miraculous signs were done by the apostles. All the believers were together and had everything in common. Selling their possessions and goods, they gave to anyone as he had need. Every day they continued to meet together in the temple courts. They broke bread in their homes and ate together with glad and sincere hearts, praising God and enjoying the favour of all the people. And the Lord added to their number daily those who were being saved (Acts 2:42–47).

A LEARNING CHURCH

The first characteristic Luke selects is very surprising; I do not think we would have chosen it. It is that a living church is a learning church. 'They devoted themselves to the apostles' teaching' (verse 42).

One might say that the Holy Spirit opened a school in Jerusalem that day. The school teachers were the apostles, whom Jesus had ap-pointed and trained, and there were three thousand pupils in the kindergarten! It was a very remarkable situation.

Wherever the Spirit of truth is at work, truth matters.

We note that those new Spirit-filled converts were not enjoying a mystical experience which led them to neglect their intellect, despise theology or stop thinking. On the contrary, 'they met constantly to hear the apostles teach' (REB). So I do not hesitate to say that anti-intellectualism and the fullness of the Holy Spirit are mutually incompatible. For who is the Holy Spirit? He is 'the Spirit of Truth'; that was one of Jesus' favourite descriptions of him. It stands to reason, therefore, that wherever the Spirit of truth is at work, truth matters.

Notice something else about those first Christian believers. They did not suppose that, because they had received the Holy Spirit, he was the only teacher they needed, and they could dispense with human teachers. Not at all. They acknowledged that Jesus had called the apostles to be the teachers of the church. So they sat at the apostles' feet. They were eager to learn all they could. And they submitted to the apostles' authority which, incidentally, was authenticated by miracles. For if verse 42 alludes to the teaching of the apostles, verse 43 refers to their many signs and wonders; indeed the main purpose of miracles throughout Scripture was to authenticate each fresh stage of revelation, especially the prophets in the Old Testament and the apostles in the New. Thus the apostle Paul could refer to his miracles as 'the signs of a true apostle' (2 Corinthians 12:12, RSV).

A living church is a learning church.

What then is the application of all this to us? How is it possible for us to submit ourselves and our churches to the teaching authority of the apostles? For we must insist that there are no apostles in the church today. To be sure, there are bishops and superintendents, church planters and pioneer missionaries, and perhaps we could call their ministries 'apostolic', giving them the adjective. But we would be wise to reserve the noun for the Twelve, Paul and perhaps James. At least my Pentecostal friends, some of whom claim the title 'apostle', agree with me that there is nobody in the church today (nor has been since the apostle John died) who has an authority comparable to that of the apostles Paul, John, Peter and James. If there were, we would have to add their teaching to that of the New Testament.

The early church understood this well. Take Ignatius, Bishop of Syrian Antioch, whose death scholars date at about 110 AD. Condemned to death as a Christian, he was travelling to Rome to be executed, and during his voyage he wrote seven or more letters to such churches as those in Rome, Ephesus, Smyrna and Tralles, in which he several times expressed this conviction: 'I do not issue you with commands like Peter and Paul, for they were apostles; I am but a condemned man.' He was a bishop, one of the earliest evidences of the rise of the monarchical episcopate, but he was not an apostle.

So I repeat my question. If there are no apostles comparable to Peter or Paul in the church today, how can we submit to apostolic teaching authority? The answer is obvious. The teaching of the apostles is found in the New Testament. It is here that their teaching has been bequeathed to us in its definitive form. This is the true 'apostolic succession', namely a continuity of apostolic doctrine, made possible by the New Testament.

Something similar was stated by the bishops of the Anglican Communion during their 1958 Lambeth Conference. In their statement on the Bible they wrote:

> The church is not 'over' the Holy Scriptures, but 'under' them, in the sense that the process of canonization was not one whereby the church conferred authority on the books, but one whereby the church acknowledged them to possess authority.

And why? The books were recognized as giving the witness of the apostles to the life, teaching, death and resurrection of the Lord and the interpretation by the apostles of these events. To that apostolic authority the church must ever bow.[1]

So we affirm first of all that a living church is a learning church, a church submissive to the teaching authority of the apostles. Its pastors expound Scripture from the pulpit. Its parents teach their children out of the Scriptures at home, and its members read and reflect on the Scriptures every day in order to grow in Christian discipleship. The Spirit of God leads the people of God to honour the word of God. Fidelity to the teaching of the apostles is the first mark of an authentic and living church.

A CARING CHURCH

If the first mark of a living church is study, the second is fellowship. 'They devoted themselves ... to the fellowship'. 'Fellowship' is the well-known Greek word *koinonia* which expresses our common (*koinos*) Christian life, what we share as believers. As we will see more fully in chapter 5, *koinonia* bears witness to two complementary truths: both what we share *in* together and what we share *out* together. And it is on this latter that Luke lays his emphasis here:

> All the believers were together and had everything in common (*koina*). Selling their possessions and goods, they gave to anyone as he had need (Acts 2:44–45).

These are disturbing verses, the kind we jump over rather quickly. What do they mean? Do they teach that every living church will become a monastic community and that every Spirit-filled believer will follow the example of the first believers literally?

A few miles east of Jerusalem at that time the Essene leaders of the Qumran Community were committed to the common ownership of their property, and new members handed over all their money and possessions when they were initiated. So then, did Jesus intend all his disciples to follow their example, selling their property and possessions and sharing the proceeds? The Anabaptists of the sixteenth-century 'Radical Reformation' talked much about Acts 2:44–45 and 4:32–37 and 'the community of goods', although only the Hutterite Brethren in eighteenth-century Moravia made common ownership compulsory.

Certainly Jesus calls some of his disciples to total voluntary poverty. This was evidently the calling of the Rich Young Ruler in the Gospels, whom Jesus told 'sell everything you have and give to the poor' (Mark 10:21). This was also the vocation of Francis of Assisi, and of Mother Teresa and her sisters – perhaps in order to witness to the world that a human life does not consist in the abundance of our possessions (see Luke 12:15).

But not all the followers of Jesus are called to this. The prohibition of private property is a Marxist, not a Christian, doctrine. Besides, even in Jerusalem the selling and the giving were voluntary. We read in verse 46 that 'they broke bread in their homes'. In their homes? But I thought they had sold their homes together with their furniture and their possessions? No, apparently not. Some still had homes in which they met. And when we come to the story of Ananias and Sapphira in Acts 5, their sin was not greed but deceit. They kept back part of the proceeds of their sale, while pretending to give it all. The apostle Peter was clear about the situation: 'Didn't it belong to you before it was sold?' And after it was sold, wasn't the money at your disposal?' (Acts 5:4). Just so all Christians have to make a conscientious decision before God what to do with our money and our possessions.

Generosity has always been a characteristic of the people of God.

Nevertheless, although we may breathe a sigh of relief that we have not been called to total poverty, we must not avoid the challenge of these verses. Those early Christians loved one another, which is hardly surprising since the first fruit of the Spirit is love (Galatians 5:22). In particular, they cared for their poor sisters and brothers, and so shared their goods with them. This principle of voluntary Christian sharing is surely a permanent one. According to UN statistics, the number of destitute people (who survive on less than 1 US dollar a day) is about 1,000 million, while the average number who die every day of hunger and hunger-related causes, is said to be about 24,000. How can we live with these statistics? Many of the poor are our brothers and sisters. The Holy Spirit gives his people a tender social conscience. So those of us who live in affluent circumstances must simplify our economic lifestyle – not because we imagine this will solve the world's macro-economic problems, but out of solidarity with the poor.

So then a living church is a caring church. Generosity has always been a characteristic of the people of God. Our God is a generous God; his church must be generous too.

A WORSHIPPING CHURCH

The third characteristic of the early church was its worship. They devoted themselves (literally) 'to the breaking of the bread' (surely a reference to the Eucharist or Lord's Supper, though probably with a fellowship meal included) 'and to the prayers', meaning not private prayer, but prayer meetings and prayer services. What strikes me about this summary of the early church's worship is its balance in two respects.

First, their worship was both formal and informal. According to verse 46 'they continued to meet together in the temple courts' and 'they broke bread in their homes'. We note therefore that they did not immediately abandon the institutional church. Doubtless they became anxious to reform it according to the gospel. And already they understood that the sacrifices of the temple had been fulfilled in the sacrifice of Christ. But they continued to attend the traditional prayer services of the temple (see Acts 3:1), which had a degree of formality, and they supplemented these with the more informal meetings in their homes, which evidently included their own distinctively Christian worship, the Eucharist.

There is an important lesson to learn here. Young people tend to be impatient with the inherited structures of the church. Understandably so, for some churches are too conservative, too resistant to change. One might say that they are stuck in the mud, and the mud has set like concrete. Their favourite formula seems to be 'As it was in the beginning, is now, and ever shall be, world without end, Amen'. We must of course listen to young people. But the Holy Spirit's way with the institution of the church is more the way of patient reform than of impatient rejection. So don't let's polarize between the structured and the unstructured. If I may general-ize, older people prefer the more formal and dignified services in the church, whereas younger people prefer the more spontaneous and liber-ated meetings in the home. We need to experience each other's preferences. The early church had both, and we need both. Every church of any size should break itself down into small fellowship groups (see chapter 5).

The early church's worship was both joyful and reverent.

Secondly, the early church's worship was both joyful and reverent. There is no doubt of their joy. The Greek word at the end of verse 46 is *agalliasis*, which is an exuberant expression of joy. God had sent his Son into the world, and now he had sent his Spirit into their hearts. How could they not be joyful? 'The fruit of the Spirit is ... joy', and sometimes a more uninhibited joy than our ecclesiastical traditions encourage.

When I attend some church services, I almost think I have come to a funeral by mistake. Everybody is dressed in black. Nobody talks or smiles. The hymns are played at the pace of a snail or a tortoise, and the whole atmosphere is lugubrious. If I could overcome my Anglo-Saxon reserve, I would want to shout 'cheer up!'. Christianity is a joyful religion, and every service should be a celebration. I am told that Archbishop Geoffrey Fisher said before he died: 'The longer I live, the more convinced I am that Christianity is one long shout of joy!'

At the same time the early church's worship was never irreverent. Yet today, if some church services are funereal, others are flippant. But if joy should characterize our worship, so should reverence. So Luke writes; 'Everyone was filled with awe' (verse 43). The living and holy God had visited Jerusalem. God was in their midst, and they bowed down before him in that mixture of wonder and humility which we call worship.

Thus the early church's worship was both formal and informal, both joyful and reverent. We need to recover this biblical balance in our Christian worship today.

AN EVANGELIZING CHURCH

So far we have considered the study, the fellowship and the worship of the early church, for it is to these three activities that Luke says 'they devoted themselves'. Yet these three are aspects of the church's interior life. They tell us nothing about its compassionate outreach to the world.

This illustrates the great danger of textual preaching, that is, of isolating a text from its context. Millions of sermons

have been preached on Acts 2:42 as if it gave a comprehensive account of the church. But on its own verse 42
presents a disastrously unbalanced picture. It gives the
impression that the early church was interested only in
studying at the feet of the apostles, caring for its own
members, and worshipping God. In other words it was
living in a ghetto, preoccupied with its own domestic life,
and ignoring the plight of the lost and the lonely outside.

But this was not the case. They were also committed to
mission, although it is not until verse 47 that we learn this.
Verse 47 corrects the imbalance of verse 42, for verse 47
implies that they were engaged in evangelism: 'And the Lord
added to their number daily those who were being saved.'
This verse teaches us three truths about the early church's
evangelism.

First, the Lord himself (that is, the Lord Jesus) did it.
Doubtless he did it through the preaching of the apostles,
the everyday witness of church members, and their common
life of love. But he did it. For he is the head of the church.
And although he delegates to pastors the responsibility
of admitting people into the visible church by baptism,
he reserves the prerogative of admitting people into the
invisible church by faith. In our self-confident age we need
to return to this truth. Only the Lord Jesus Christ by his
Holy Spirit can open the eyes of the blind and give life to
dead souls, and so add people to his church. We need
humbly to acknowledge this.

Secondly, the Lord did two things together. He 'added to
their number . . . those who were being saved'. He didn't add
them to the church without saving them, and he didn't save

them without adding them to the church. Salvation and church membership went together; they still do.

Thirdly, the Lord did both these things 'daily', or day by day. Those early Christians did not regard evangelism as an occasional activity. They were not content to organize a quinquennial mission. No, their witness was as continuous as their worship. And the Lord honoured it. Converts were being added daily.

We urgently need to return to this eager expectation. I know some churches which haven't had a convert for ten years or more. And if they got one, they wouldn't know what to do with him, her or it, so extraordinary would this phenomenon appear to them! But the early church anticipated the arrival of new believers, and made provision for their nurture.

Looking back over the four essential marks of a living church, it is apparent that they all have to do with the believers' relationships.

First, they were related to the apostles. They devoted themselves to the apostles' teaching. A living church is an apostolic church.

Secondly, they were related to each other. They loved each other. A living church is a caring and sharing church.

Thirdly, they were related to God. They worshipped God in the breaking of bread and in prayers, with joy and with reverence. A living church is a worshipping church.

Fourthly, they were related to the world outside. They reached out in witness. A living church is an evangelizing church.

Some years ago, visiting a large Latin American city, I was told of a group of Christian students who had dropped out of the church and called themselves *Cristianos descolgados*, 'unhooked Christians'. The reason they had dropped out was their disillusionment with the churches in their city. They lacked biblical teaching, social concern, authentic worship and compassionate outreach, in fact the very marks which the early church exhibited and young people are looking for today.

A living church is an evangelizing church.

We don't have to wait for the Holy Spirit to come, for he did come on the Day of Pentecost, and he has never left the church. Indeed, there is a sense in which the Day of Pentecost cannot be repeated, any more than Christmas Day, Good Friday, Easter Day and Ascension Day can be repeated. For Jesus was born once, died once, rose once, ascended once and sent the Holy Spirit once. But what we do need to do is to humble ourselves before God, and seek the fullness, the direction and the power of the Holy Spirit. For then our churches will at least approximate to the essentials of a living church in apostolic doctrine, loving fellowship, joyful worship and outgoing, ongoing evangelism.

Chapter 2

WORSHIP:
GLORYING IN
GOD'S HOLY NAME

It is often said that the church's pre-eminent responsibility is evangelism. But this is not so, for at least three reasons. First, evangelism comes under the heading of our duty to our neighbour, whereas worship is our duty to God, and our duty to God must take precedence over our duty to our neighbour.

Secondly, although all of us are expected to share the gospel with others whenever the opportunity presents itself, evangelism is also a spiritual gift or *charisma* (Ephesians 4:11) which is given only to some. Thus not all Christians are evangelists, but all Christians are worshippers, both in private and in public.

Thirdly, evangelism is a temporary activity, which will cease when the Lord Jesus comes to consummate his kingdom. But our worship will continue throughout eternity.

This being so, namely that worship is the church's pre-eminent duty, we should surely give it our closest attention.

What, however, is worship? Of course, the whole of our life is worship, serving God with all our being. But how shall we define it? Perhaps the best scriptural definition is to be found in Psalm 105:3. To worship is to 'glory in God's holy name'. God's name is his revealed character. It is 'holy' because it is unique, set apart from and above all other names. And once we glimpse the holiness of God's great name, we see the fitness of 'glorying' or revelling in it. Indeed, we are to join with all creatures in pronouncing him worthy of our praise, because he is both our Creator and our Redeemer (Revelation 5:9–14). Because of who God is, it is appropriate that we should 'worship at his footstool' (Psalm 99:5).

Worship is the church's pre-eminent duty.

True worship according to Scripture has four main characteristics.

BIBLICAL WORSHIP

First, true worship is biblical worship, that is to say, it is a response to the biblical revelation. We no doubt remember how the apostle Paul found in Athens an altar inscribed 'to an unknown god'. Paul went on to claim that what the philosophers worshipped as unknown he was going to proclaim to them (Acts 17:23). The truth is that it is impossible to worship an unknown god. For if we do not know him, we cannot worship him, and our so-called worship is bound to degenerate into idolatry.

So Christian worship could be defined as 'a response to revelation'. Hence the reading and preaching of God's word in public worship, far from being alien intrusions into it, are rather indispensable aspects of it. It is the word of God which evokes the worship of God. So the sixteenth-century Anglican reformers provided in the Prayer Book both a church calendar and a corresponding lectionary, that is, a table of set lessons for every Sunday of the year. They rightly swept away all unbiblical legends, which had been popular in the middle ages, and they retained only biblical prayers.

It is a good and healthy custom either to encourage members of the congregation to bring their Bibles with them to church, or to provide Bibles in the seats. Then, when the text of the lessons and the sermon is announced, there is a great rustling of pages as people find the place and follow the text.

When this happens, the situation is similar to the time when Cornelius the centurion received the apostle Peter into his home. He said to Peter: 'Now we are all here in the presence of God to listen to everything the Lord has commanded you to tell us' (Acts 10:33).

This spirit of receptivity is a necessary condition of hearing the word of God. So much depends on how the readers and preachers approach their task.

It is a great privilege to read the lessons in church. I was fortunate enough while still at school to be commissioned to be a lesson-reader in chapel. One day an elderly Christian man, on hearing that I read the lessons, shared with me the lesson-reader's text, namely Nehemiah 8:8 (RV): 'And they read in the book, in the law of God, distinctly; and they gave the sense, so that they understood the reading.'

More privileged still than those who read God's word are those who are commissioned to preach it. It goes without saying that preachers are expositors; their task is to open up, explain and apply Scripture. (This is the subject of chapter 6.)

Since our worship is a response to God's word, its mood must be modulated according to the nature of the truth being expounded.

Our worship is a response to God's word.

Take Psalm 95 as an example. It is an exhortation to the people of God to praise him, but it contains an abrupt change of mood in the middle. The psalm begins with a call to sing for joy to the Lord and to shout aloud to the Rock of our salvation. Why? Because 'the LORD is the great God', the creator of earth and sea. Then in verse 6 the mood changes, and we are summoned to bow down and kneel before the Lord. Why? Because he is our God, and we are 'the people of his pasture; the flock under his care'. Thus there is a place in public worship both for shouting aloud because he is the *great* God, and for bowing down before him because he is *our* God. It is a mistake, therefore, to sing all our hymns and songs *fortissimo*, as if the Holy Spirit's presence is to be measured by decibels. For it is sometimes more appropriate for the music to be *piano*, and even *pianissimo*, varying the volume according to the subject.

CONGREGATIONAL WORSHIP

Secondly, true worship is congregational worship. Of course some people still tell us that they find it easier to worship God on their own than in a crowd. And certainly there is a place for private and individual worship, even in the Psalter. But the Psalmist focuses more on corporate worship. For example, 'Praise, O servants of the LORD' (Psalm 113:1) and 'Sing to the LORD a new song, his praise in the assembly of the saints' (Psalm 149:1). And in the New Testament we read this exhortation:

> *Worship which is pleasing to God is offered by his people together.*

> Let us not give up meeting, as some are in the habit of doing, but let us encourage one another – and all the more as you see the Day approaching (Hebrews 10:25).

Moreover, the worship which is pleasing to God is offered by his people together, who have assembled in order to do so. The Reformers understood the implications of this principle, namely that everybody should participate. Whereas the medieval mass was celebrated by the priest at the high altar, and the lay people were spectators, the

Reformers deliberately brought the action down from the chancel to the nave and ensured that the lay people were not merely spectators but participants.

Further, whereas the medieval mass was said in Latin, the Reformers insisted on the use of the vernacular. The Anglican Article 24 could hardly be more explicit:

> It is a thing plainly repugnant to the Word of God, and the custom of the primitive church, to have public prayer in the church, or to minister the sacraments in a tongue not understanded of the people.

Yet the Roman Catholic Church retained the use of Latin until the provisions of the Second Vatican Council (1965).

Archbishop Cranmer was concerned that his Prayer Book would be a 'Book of *Common* Prayer'. He ensured lay participation in the different services by including some forms which the congregation would say together – for example the General Confession, the Lord's Prayer, the Apostles' Creed, the Gloria, the General Thanksgiving and the Prayer of Humble Access. True, such prayers and other forms can degenerate into a mere recitation, but during extempore prayer the mind can also wander. Probably the best and safest way is to combine liturgical and spontaneous prayer, and to replace a monopoly by one leader with different participants – in music, lesson-reading, intercessions and preaching.

Our common congregational worship should clearly express the international, intercultural character of the body of Christ. For example, throughout his Roman letter the apostle was conscious of the tensions which existed in the church between Jews and Gentiles. So in chapter 15 he prayed that God might give them 'a spirit of unity' among themselves, in order that they might engage in the common worship of God 'so that with one heart and mouth' they might glorify the God and Father of our Lord Jesus Christ (Romans 15:5–6).

This issue of united trans-cultural worship has recently come to the surface in the debate about the so-called 'homogeneous unit principle' (HUP). It was developed by the late Dr Donald McGavran, the founder of the Fuller School of World Mission and Church Growth. In his book *Understanding Church Growth* (1970) he stated the principle thus, that 'people like to become Christians without crossing racial, linguistic or class barriers'. This HUP is an observable fact. And many people go further and argue that it is legitimate in evangelism to focus on particular people-groups.

But if the HUP is legitimate in evangelism, is it also legitimate in the church? This is where the debate erupted. Should we tolerate, let alone welcome, HUP churches, that is, churches whose members all belong to an identical and particular culture? Surely not. For the Lord Jesus has broken down the barriers between Jews and Gentiles, men and women, slaves and free. How then can we erect fresh barriers in the only community in which Christ has abolished them?

An important international colloquium on this topic took place in Pasadena, California, in 1977, in which five faculty members of Fuller's School of World Mission met and debated with their critics. Its report was entitled 'The Pasadena Statement on the Homogeneous Unit Principle'.[1]

All participants affirmed both the fundamental unity of the church and the colourful diversity of culture. But the question was how to reconcile them. We felt able to say that, although there are circumstances in which a homogeneous church can be a legitimate and authentic church, yet it can never be a complete church in itself, since it cannot reflect the universality and diversity of the body of Christ. This being so, every homogeneous unit church should take active steps to broaden its fellowship, in order to demonstrate visibly the unity and variety of the church. For example, a large city church should break itself down into several homogeneous unit churches or sub-churches, so that they can celebrate both separately and together.

Every church should demonstrate visibly the unity and variety of the church.

In particular, we should all be inspired by the eschatological vision of the great multitude which no one can count, from every nation, tribe, people and language, redeemed and standing before God's throne (Revelation 7:9–10). The Lord's Supper should be a dramatic foreshadowing of the Messianic banquet of the kingdom of God.

SPIRITUAL WORSHIP

Thirdly, true worship is spiritual worship. Scripture often emphasizes that true worship is not in itself a matter of forms, rituals and ceremonies. We need to listen carefully to the biblical criticism of religion. No book, not even by Marx and his followers, is more scathing of empty religion than the Bible. The prophets of the eighth and seventh century BC were outspoken in their denunciation of the formalism and hypocrisy of Israelite worship. Jesus then applied their critique to the Pharisees of his day: 'These people . . . honour me with their lips, but their hearts are far from me' (Isaiah 29:13; Mark 7:6). And this indictment of religion by the Old Testament prophets and by Jesus is uncomfortably applicable to us and some of our churches today. Too much of our worship is ritual without reality, form without power, fun without fear, religion without God. Nobody has expressed this with more mischievous sarcasm than Malcolm Muggeridge:

> One of the most effective defensive systems against God's incursions has hitherto been organised religion. The various churches have provided a refuge for fugitives from God – his voice drowned in the chanting, his smell lost in the incense, his purpose obscured and confused in creeds, dogmas, dissertations and other priestly pronunciamentos. In vast cathedrals, as in little conventicles, or just wrapped in Quaker silence, one could get away from God. Plainsong held him at bay, as did revivalist eloquence, hearty hymns and intoned prayers. Confronted with that chanting, moaning, gurgling voice – 'Dearly beloved brethren, I pray and beseech you . . .' or with that earnest, open Oxfam face, shining like the morning sun with all the glories flesh is heir to, God could be relied on to make off.[2]

At this point something more needs to be said about the place of music in public worship. For both vocal and instrumental music can be a wonderful vehicle for the praise of God, but can also provoke him to cry: 'Away with the noise of your songs! I will not listen to the music of your harps' (Amos 5:23).

It seems that in every generation there has been a flowering of gifted musicians who have brought their talent to the service of God. Jewish praise was enriched by singing and a whole variety of musical instruments (see Psalm 150). So it has also been with Christian worship, whether we are thinking of the sonorous organ in a medieval cathedral, or brass, strings and wind in Lutheran devotion, or the guitar, the saxophone and the drums today. I have no intention of pronouncing between classical and contemporary music, for different styles appeal to different temperaments and cultures. What is essential, however, is the biblical content of the hymns and songs. Then we shall avoid excessive repetition, which can easily degenerate into the 'babbling' which Jesus condemned in the Sermon on the Mount (*battalogia* in Matthew 6:7). *Battalogia* seems to denote any speech in which the mouth is engaged but the mind is not.

The vocation of the church to offer God spiritual worship is of special importance today. For even in the 'secular' west there is a widespread hunger for 'spirituality'.

The most striking of all recent religious trends is the rise of the New Age movement. It is a bizarre assortment of diverse beliefs – of religion and science, physics and metaphysics, ancient pantheism and evolutionary optimism, astrology, spiritism, reincarnation, ecology and alternative medicine. In sum, it is a recognition that materialism cannot satisfy the human spirit, and a search for another, transcendent reality. People are seeking it everywhere.

This quest for transcendence is a challenge to us and to the quality of our public worship. Does it offer what people are craving – the element of mystery, the 'sense of the numenous'; in biblical language 'the fear of God', in modern language 'transcendence'? My answer to my own question is 'Not often'. The church is not always conspicuous for the profound reality of its worship. In particular, we who call ourselves 'evangelical' do not know much how to worship. Evangelism is our speciality, not worship. We seem to have little sense of the greatness and glory of Almighty God. We do not bow down before him in awe and wonder. Our tendency is to be cocky, flippant and proud. We take little trouble to prepare our worship services. In consequence, they

We do not know much how to worship.

are sometimes slovenly, mechanical, perfunctory and dull. At other times they are frivolous, to the point of irreverence. No wonder those seeking reality often pass us by!

What is needed, then? Here are some suggestions. First, we need such a faithful reading and preaching of God's word that through it his living voice is heard addressing his people again. Secondly, we need such a reverent and expectant administration of the Eucharist or Lord's Supper that (I choose my words carefully) there is a Real Presence of Jesus Christ. His presence is not in the elements, but among his people and at his table, Jesus Christ himself objectively and really present, coming to meet us, ready to make himself known to us through the breaking of bread, and anxious to give himself to us, so that we may feed on him in our hearts by faith. Thirdly, we need such a sincere offering of praise and prayer, that God's people say with Jacob, 'Surely the LORD is in this place, and I was not aware of it' (Genesis 28:16), and unbelievers present will fall down and worship God, exclaiming 'God is really among you!' (1 Corinthians 14:24–25).

In brief, it is a great tragedy that many of our contemporaries, who are seeking transcendence, turn to drugs, sex, yoga, cults, mysticism, the New Age and science fiction, instead of to the church, in whose worship services true transcendence should always be experienced, and a close encounter with the living God enjoyed.

MORAL WORSHIP

The kind of worship which is pleasing to God has one more major characteristic. True worship is moral worship, that is to say, it must not only express what is in our hearts but also be accompanied by an upright life. Samuel put this beyond doubt in his explicit words to King Saul: 'To obey is better than sacrifice, and to heed is better than the fat of rams' (1 Samuel 15:22).

God was even more outspoken in his declaration to Isaiah. He had had enough of Israel's offerings. He took no pleasure in their sacrifices. Indeed, their sacred assemblies were an abomination to him, and he would not even listen to their prayers. Why so? He tells them: 'Your hands are full of blood'. If they would 'stop doing wrong, and seek justice, encourage the oppressed', they would be forgiven (Isaiah 1:10–19). It was this mixture of religion, wrongdoing and injustice which God could not abide. Worship without holiness was hateful to him.

I cannot think of a better place to conclude this chapter on worship than at the beginning of Romans 12. For here Paul describes the Christian life to which he summons us as our 'spiritual act of worship'.

For eleven chapters the apostle has been unfolding 'the mercies of God'. And now, in view of God's great mercy which we have received, he appeals to all the members of God's international family to present our bodies as living sacrifices to God. He calls this physical offering our 'spiritual' act of worship. *Logikos* is the word he uses, which could be translated either 'reasonable' (logical in response to God's mercy) or 'rational' (intelligent, the offering of heart and mind, spiritual as opposed to ceremonial).

Worship without holiness is hateful to [God].

It is clear that Paul is thinking of a worship which is expressed not only in a church building but in the home and in the workplace. One kind of worship is unbalanced without the other.

Chapter 3

EVANGELISM:
MISSION THROUGH
THE LOCAL CHURCH

We should be very grateful to the African bishops for pro-
posing, and to the other bishops for agreeing, that the last ten
years of the twentieth century, indeed of the second millen-
nium AD, should be declared 'A Decade of Evangelism'.

This decision of the 1988 Lambeth Conference brought
evangelism to the top of the Anglican church's agenda and
challenged us to ask ourselves what we know and believe
about evangelism. For the whole Anglican Communion
found itself obliged to face a responsibility which it has often
shirked, namely the call to bear witness to Jesus Christ.

According to the definition which the Anglican primates
commended to us, to evangelize is 'to make known by word
and deed the love of the crucified and risen Christ in the
power of the Holy Spirit, so that people will repent, believe

and receive Christ as their Saviour and obediently serve him as their Lord in the fellowship of his church.'[1]

Not that evangelism is foreign to the ethos of Anglicanism. Far from it. The *Second Book of Homilies*, for example, written mostly by Bishop John Jewel of Salisbury, and published in 1571, contains the following admonition: 'If any man be a dumb Christian, not professing his faith openly, but cloaking and colouring himself for fear of danger in time to come, he giveth men occasion, justly and with good conscience, to doubt lest he have not the grace of the Holy Ghost within him, because he is tongue tied and doth not speak.'

FORMS OF EVANGELISM

Evangelism can of course take different forms. Ever since Jesus offered living water to the Samaritan woman at Jacob's well (John 4:4–15), and Philip sat beside the Ethiopian in his chariot and told him the good news of Jesus (Acts 8:26–35), *personal evangelism* has had impeccable biblical precedents. It is still our duty, when the opportunity is given and in a spirit of humility, to share Christ with those of our relatives, friends, neighbours and colleagues who do not yet know him.

Mass evangelism too (the preaching of an evangelist to crowds) has over the centuries been signally blessed by God. The recent disgracing of a few American televangelists does not contradict this fact. Besides, Jesus himself proclaimed the good news of the kingdom to the crowds in Galilee. So did the apostle Paul to the pagans of Lystra (Acts 14:14–18) and the philosophers of Athens (Acts 17:22–23), and

Wesley and Whitefield in eighteenth-century Britain and America. Gifted evangelists of many nationalities are still preaching effectively to large crowds today, although they know that their ministry depends on the active cooperation of churches and Christians. And all over the world there are clergy and lay people who take their preaching seriously, and who remember that in their congregation there will often be both non-Christians and nominal Christians who need to hear the gospel.

Nevertheless, *local church evangelism* can claim to be the most normal, natural and productive method of spreading the gospel today.[2] There are two main reasons for commending it.

First, there is the argument from Scripture. According to the apostle Peter, the church is both 'a royal priesthood' to offer spiritual sacrifices to God (which is worship) and 'a holy nation' to spread abroad God's praises (which is witness) (1 Peter 2:9–10). Moreover, these responsibilities of the universal church devolve on each local church. Every Christian congregation is called by God to be a worshipping, witnessing community. Indeed, each of these two duties necessarily involves the other. If we truly worship God, acknowledging and adoring his infinite worth, we find ourselves impelled to make him known to others, in order that they may worship him too. Thus worship leads to

> *Worship leads to witness, and witness to worship.*

witness, and witness in its turn to worship, in a perpetual circle.

The Thessalonians set a fine example of local church evangelism. Near the beginning of his first letter to them Paul points out this remarkable sequence: 'Our gospel came to you ... You welcomed the message ... The Lord's message rang out from you' (1 Thessalonians 1:5–6, 8). In this way the local church becomes like a sounding board which reflects and amplifies the vibrations it receives, or like a radio station which first accepts and then transmits a message. Every church which has heard the gospel must pass it on. This is still God's principal method of evangelism. If all churches had been faithful, the world would long ago have been evangelized.

Secondly, there is the argument from strategy. Each local church is situated in a particular neighbourhood. Its first mission responsibility must therefore be to the people who live there. The congregation is strategically placed to reach the area around it. Any political party would be wildly jealous of the buildings and personnel which are at our disposal. The churches in many countries have ample resources to disseminate the gospel throughout their land.

Thus biblical theology and practical strategy combine to make the local church the primary agent of evangelism.

But if the local church is to act out its God-appointed role, it must first fulfil four conditions. It must *understand* itself (the theology of the church), *organize* itself (the structures of the church), *express* itself (the message of the church), and *be* itself (the life of the church).

THE CHURCH MUST UNDERSTAND ITSELF: ITS THEOLOGY

I make no apology for beginning with theology. Many churches are sick because they have a false self-image. They have grasped neither who they are (their identity) nor what they are called to be (their vocation). We all know the importance for mental health of having an accurate self-image. What is true of persons is equally true of churches.

At least two false images of the church are prevalent today.

The first false image is *the religious club* (or *introverted Christianity*). According to this view, the local church somewhat resembles the local golf club, except that the common interest of its members happens to be God rather than golf. They see themselves as religious people who enjoy doing religious things together. They pay their subscription and reckon that they are entitled to certain privileges. In fact, they concentrate on the status and advantages of being club members. They have evidently forgotten (or never known) the perceptive dictum attributed to Archbishop William Temple that 'the church is the only co-operative society in the world which exists for the benefit of its non-members'. Instead, they are completely introverted, like an ingrown toe-nail. To be sure, Temple was guilty of a slight exaggeration, for church members do have a responsibility to each other, as the many 'one another' verses

Many churches have a false self-image.

of the New Testament indicate ('love one another', 'encourage one another', 'bear one another's burdens', etc.). Nevertheless, our primary responsibilities are our worship of God and our mission in the world.

At the opposite extreme to the religious club is *the secular mission* (or *religionless Christianity*). It was in the 1960s that some Christian thinkers became understandably exasperated by what they saw as the ecclesiastical self-centredness of the church. The church seemed to them so incorrigibly absorbed in its own petty domestic affairs that they resolved to abandon it and drop out. For the arena of divine service they exchanged the church for the secular city. They were no longer interested in 'worship services', they said, but only in 'worship service'. So they tried to develop a 'religionless Christianity' in which they re-interpreted worship as mission, love for God as love for neighbour, and prayer to God as encounter with people.

How, some forty years later, should we evaluate this movement? We must surely agree that their distaste for selfish religion was right. Since it is nauseating to God, it ought to sicken us also. But the concept of a 'religionless Christianity' was an unbalanced over-reaction. We have no liberty to confuse worship and mission, even though (as we have seen) each involves the other. There is always an element of mission in worship and of worship in mission, but they are not synonymous.

There is a third way to understand the church, which combines what is true in both false images, and which recognizes that we have a responsibility both to worship God and to serve the world. This is *the double identity of the church* (or *incarnational Christianity*). By its 'double identity' I mean that the church is a people who have been both called out of the world to worship God and sent back into the world to witness and serve. These are, in fact, two of the classical 'marks' of the church. According to the first, the church is 'holy', called out to belong to God and to worship him. According to the second, the church is 'apostolic', sent out into the world on its mission. Alternatively, we may say that the church is summoned by God to be simultaneously 'holy' (distinct from the world) and 'worldly' (not in the sense of assimilating the world's values and standards, but in the sense of renouncing other-worldliness and becoming instead immersed in the life of the world). It was Dr Alec Vidler who admirably captured the church's double identity by referring to its 'holy worldliness'.[3]

Nobody has ever exhibited the meaning of 'holy worldliness' better than our Lord Jesus Christ himself. His incarnation is the perfect embodiment of it. On the one hand he came to us in our world, and assumed the full reality of our humanness. He made himself one with us in our frailty, and exposed himself to our temptations. He fraternized with the common people, and they flocked round him eagerly. He welcomed everybody and shunned nobody. He identified himself with our sorrows, our sins and our death. On the other hand, in mixing freely with people like us, he never sacrificed, or even for one moment compromised, his own unique identity. His was the perfection of 'holy worldliness'.

And now he sends us into the world as he was sent into the world (John 17:18; 20:21). We have to penetrate other people's worlds, as he penetrated ours: the world of their thinking (as we struggle to understand their misunderstandings of the gospel), the world of their feeling (as we try to empathize with their pain), and the world of their living (as we sense the humiliation of their social situation, whether poverty, homelessness, unemployment or discrimination). Archbishop Michael Ramsey put it well when he wrote in his critique of secular theology: 'we state and commend the faith only in so far as we go out and put ourselves with loving sympathy inside the doubts of the doubter, the questions of the questioner, and the loneliness of those who have lost the way'.[4] Yet this costly entry into other people's worlds is not to be undertaken at the cost of our own Christian integrity. We are called to maintain the standards of Jesus Christ untarnished.

The church [has a] God-given double identity.

Seldom in its long history has the church managed to preserve its God-given double identity of holy worldliness. Instead, it has tended to oscillate between the two extremes. Sometimes (in an over-emphasis on its holiness) the church has withdrawn from the world and so has neglected its mission. At other times (in an over-emphasis on its worldliness) it has conformed to the world, assimilating its views and values, and so has neglected its holiness. But in order to fulfil its mission, the church must faithfully respond to both its callings and preserve both parts of its identity.

'Mission' arises, then, from the biblical doctrine of the church in the world. If we are not 'the church', the holy and distinct people of God, we have nothing to say because we are compromised. If, on the other hand, we are not 'in the world', deeply involved in its life and suffering, we have no one to serve because we are insulated. Our calling is to be 'holy' and 'worldly' at the same time. Without this balanced biblical ecclesiology we will never recover or fulfil our mission.

THE CHURCH MUST ORGANIZE ITSELF: ITS STRUCTURES

The church must organize itself in such a way as to express its understanding of itself. Its structures must reflect its theology, especially its double identity, whether the people meet in a traditional church or chapel building, a school, theatre, pub, hall or home.

The commonest fault is for the church to be structured for 'holiness' rather than 'worldliness', for worship and fellowship rather than mission. This was the emphasis of the report *The Church for Others* (1968), sub-titled 'A Quest for Structures for Missionary Congregations'. One does not have to agree with everything in the book in order to appreciate its thrust that

the missionary church is not concerned with itself – it is a church for others ... Its centre lies outside itself; it must live 'ex-centredly' ... The church has to turn itself outwards to the world ... We have to recognize that the churches have developed into 'waiting churches' into which people are expected to come. Its inherited structures stress and embody this static outlook. One may say that we are in danger of perpetuating 'come-structures' instead of replacing them by 'go-structures'. One may say that inertia has replaced the dynamism of the gospel and of participation in the mission of God.[5]

Further, our static, inflexible, self-centred structures are 'heretical structures' because they embody a heretical doctrine of the church.

Our static, inflexible, self-centred structures are 'heretical'.

It has been very refreshing, while reading the Church of England report, *Mission-shaped Church*, to note its regular use of the expression 'missionary churches', alluding not to a particular kind of church but rather to an essential feature of every church.

Some zealous churches organize an overfull programme of church-based activities. Something is arranged for every night of the week. On Monday night the committees meet, and on Tuesday night the fellowship groups. On Wednesday night the Bible study takes place, and on Thursday night the prayer meeting. Even on Friday and Saturday evenings other good causes occupy people's time and energy. Such churches give the impression that their main goal is to keep their members out of mischief! Certainly they have neither time nor opportunity to get into mischief since they are busily engaged in the church every single night of the week!

But such a crowded, church-centred programme, admirable as it may look at first sight, has many drawbacks and dangers. To begin with, it is detrimental to Christian family life. Marriages break up and families disintegrate because father and/or mother are seldom at home. It also inhibits church members from getting involved in the local community because they are preoccupied with the local church. It thus contradicts an essential part of the church's identity, namely its 'worldliness'. As Bishop Richard Wilke of the United Methodist Church in the United States has put it, 'our structure has become an end in itself, not a means of saving the world'.[6] In that case it is a heretical structure.

Come to Christ for worship and go for Christ in mission.

I sometimes wonder (although I exaggerate in order to make my point) if it would not be very healthy for church members to meet only on Sundays (for worship, fellowship and teaching) and not at all midweek. Then we would gather on Sundays and scatter for the rest of the week. We would come to Christ for worship and go for Christ in mission. And in that rhythm of Sunday-weekday, gathering-scattering, coming-going and worship-mission the church would express its holy worldliness, and its structure would conform to its double identity.

How, then, should the local church organize itself? Ideally, it seems to me, every five or ten years each church should conduct a survey in order to evaluate itself and especially to discover how far its structures reflect its identity. In fact, it should conduct two surveys, one of the local community and the other of the local church, in order to learn how far the church is penetrating the community for Christ. This idea was taken up in Britain by ACUPA (the Archbishops' Commission on Urban Priority Areas), whose influential report was entitled *Faith in the City*. It recommended what it called a 'local church audit', consisting of both 'the church profile' ('to build up an accurate picture of the local church') and 'the parish profile' ('to build up an accurate picture of the parish').[7] Perhaps I could take these in the opposite order.

First, a local community survey, as each church is set in a particular situation, and needs to become familiar with it in all its particularity. A questionnaire will need to be drawn up. Here are some of the questions which it will probably include:

1. What sort of people live in our area? What is their ethnic origin, nationality, religion, culture, media preference, and work? Are there families, single-parent families, single people, senior citizens, young people? What are the area's main social needs, relating to housing, employment, poverty, education?
2. Has the local area any centres of education, whether schools, colleges, adult education centres, or play groups?
3. What places of business are found in it? Factories, farms, offices, shops, or studios? Is there significant unemployment?

4. Where do the people live? Do they occupy houses or flats, and do they own or rent them? Are there any hotels, hostels, student residences, apartment blocks?
5. Where do people congregate when they are at leisure? Café or restaurant, pub or nightclub, shopping mall, youth club or other clubs, bingo hall, concert hall, leisure centre, theatre or cinema, sports ground or park?
6. What public services have their headquarters locally? Police, fire brigade, prison, hospital, public library, other social services?
7. Are there other religious buildings – church or chapel, synagogue, mosque, temple, or Christian Science reading room?
8. Has the community changed in the last ten years, and what changes can be forecast during the next ten?

In the second survey, on the local church, probing questions will need to be asked. Is the church in reality organized only for itself, for its own survival and convenience, and for the preservation of its privileges? Is it organized to serve itself, or to serve God and the community? What are its cherished traditions and conventions which unnecessarily separate it from the community? The questionnaire might include the following areas:

The church building, whether traditional or contemporary, whether owned or rented. Church members tend to be most interested in its interior (its beauty, comfort and amenities). But we also need to walk round it and look at it through the eyes of an outsider. What image does it present? Is it a fortress (dark, forbidding and austere), or is it bright, inviting and welcoming?

As an illustration, let me mention visiting the huge central square of the capital city of a Latin American republic. In the middle was the statue of the national hero, who had rescued the country at the beginning of the last century from the Spanish *conquistadores*. One side of the square was entirely occupied by the Roman Catholic cathedral. I tried to get in, but it was closed. On the steps leading up to its main door, however, were three human beings – a drunk who had vomited copiously, a blind beggar selling matches, and a prostitute who was offering herself to passers-by in broad daylight. A drunk, a beggar and a prostitute, three symbols of human tragedy, and behind them a locked cathedral, which seemed to be saying 'Keep out! We don't want you.' I realize that there may have been good reasons why the cathedral was closed. My concern is with the 'vibes' which were given off by that scene.

Is the church in reality organized only for itself?

A critical look at the inside of the church building will be necessary too, especially through the eyes of non-Christian visitors – its decoration and furniture, lighting and heating, its notice boards, posters, bookstall and leaflets.

The church services. As with the first-century Jewish synagogue, so with the twenty-first century Christian church, there are 'godfearers' on the edge of every congregation, who are attracted but not yet committed to Christ. Are our worship services exclusively for the committed, designed only for the initiated, and therefore mumbo jumbo to outsiders? Or do we remember the fringe members and non-members who may be present? What about the forms of service, the liturgy and language, the music (words, tunes and instruments), the seating, and the dress of both leaders and congregation? We need to ask ourselves what messages these things proclaim.

The church membership. Is our membership mobilized for mission? Or is our church so clericalized (i.e. clergy-dominated) as to make this impossible? Has it grasped the New Testament teaching about the every-member ministry of the body of Christ? Or is it less a body than a pyramid, with the clergy at the pinnacle and the lay people in their serried ranks of inferiority at the base? Are the members of the church also members of the community? Or are they either confined to church activities or practising a commuter-Christianity (travelling long distances to church), which makes local involvement difficult, even artificial?

Do we imprison our members in the church?

The church programme. Do we imprison our members in the church? Or do we deliberately release at least some of them (including leaders) from church commitments in order to encourage them to be active for Christ in the community, and then support them with our interest and prayers as they do so? Do we ensure that the biblical truth of the double identity of the church is taught and embodied, and that training is available for those who want to commit themselves to Christian service and witness?

The two surveys (of community and church) will need to be studied by the church leadership (council, diaconate, or whatever it is called) both separately and in relation to each other. Out of this reflection will grow a strategy for mission. The leadership (preferably with others who may wish to be involved) will set both long-term and short-term goals, and establish a list of priorities. They may decide that the church is suffering from a false self-image and needs above all else some biblical teaching on its holy worldliness and on the implications of this for mission; or that a training programme must be arranged to equip members for evangelism; or that church-based activities should be reduced in order to increase members' involvement in the community. It might be decided to restructure radically the church building, decor, seating or services; or to organize a general visitation of the local area, if possible in co-operation with other local churches; or to form specialist groups to penetrate particular, secular segments of the district.

For example, a group of committed young people could adopt a local nightclub, not in order to make occasional evangelistic raids into it, but between them (in pairs) to visit it regularly over a long period, in order to make friends with the other young people who congregate there. Again, the church may decide to arrange home meetings for neighbours, or a series of apologetic lectures in a local and neutral building, or regular guest services with an evangelistic thrust, to which members would be encouraged to bring their friends. Or the church may determine to take up some special social need in the local area which has surfaced during the surveys, and encourage a group to study it and then recommend action. All such decisions will be designed to help the church to identify with the community, and to develop structures which facilitate an authentically incarnational mission.

THE CHURCH MUST EXPRESS ITSELF: ITS MESSAGE

It is not enough for the local church to understand itself and organize itself accordingly; it must also articulate its message. For evangelism, at its simplest and most basic, is sharing the *evangel*, the good news. So in order to define evangelism we must also define the good news.

The local church must also articulate its message.

There can be no doubt that the essence of the gospel is Jesus Christ himself. It would be impossible to preach the Christian good news without talking about Jesus. So we read that Philip, speaking to the Ethiopian, 'told him the good news about Jesus' (Acts 8:35), and that the apostle Paul described himself as 'set apart for the gospel of God ... regarding his Son' (Romans 1:1, 3). Moreover, in bearing witness to Jesus we must speak above all of his death and resurrection. To quote Paul again in his famous summary of the apostolic gospel, 'what I received I passed on to you as of first importance: that Christ died for our sins according to the Scriptures, that he was buried, that he was raised on the third day according to the Scriptures, and that he appeared...' (1 Corinthians 15:3–5). We simply do not share the gospel if we do not declare God's love in the gift of his Son to live our life, to die for our sins and to rise again, together with his offer through Jesus Christ, to all who repent and believe, of a new life of forgiveness and freedom, and of membership in his new society. The Anglican primates' recommended definition of the gospel includes these essentials: 'to make known by word and deed the love of the crucified and risen Christ in the power of the Holy Spirit, so that people will repent, believe and receive Christ as their Saviour and obediently serve him as their Lord in the fellowship of his church.'

But how shall we formulate this good news in our world's increasingly pluralistic societies, in such a way that it resonates with them and makes sense? There are two opposite extremes to avoid.

The first extreme I will call *total fixity*. Some Christian people seem to be in bondage to words and formulae, and so become prisoners of a gospel stereotype. They wrap up their message in a nice, neat package; they tape, label and price-tag it as if it were destined for the supermarket. Then, unless their favourite phraseology is used (whether the kingdom of God, or the blood of Jesus, or human liberation, or being born again, or justification by faith, or the cosmic lordship of Christ), they roundly declare that the gospel has not been preached. What these people seem not to have noticed is the rich diversity of gospel formulation which is found in the New Testament itself. The options I have listed are all biblical, but because all of them contain an element of imagery, and each image is different, it is impossible to fuse them into a single, simple concept. So it is perfectly legitimate to develop one or other of them, according to what seems most appropriate to the occasion.

The opposite extreme is *total fluidity*. Some years ago I heard a British bishop say: 'There's no such thing as the gospel in a vacuum. You don't even know what the gospel is until you enter each particular situation. You have to enter the situation first, and then you discover the gospel when you're there.' Now if he meant that he wanted a gospel in context, not in a vacuum, and that we need to relate the gospel sensitively to each person and situation, I am in full agreement with him; but to say 'there is no such thing as the gospel in a vacuum' and 'you discover it' in each situation is surely a serious overstatement. For what the advocates of total fluidity seem not to have noticed is that, alongside the New Testament's rich diversity of gospel formulation, there is also an underlying unity (especially regarding the saving death and resurrection of Jesus) which binds the different formulations together. As Professor A. M. Hunter wrote, 'there is ... a deep unity in the New Testament, which dominates and transcends all the diversities'.[8]

Is there a middle way? Yes, there is. Both the extremes which I have described express important concerns which need to be preserved. The first ('total fixity') rightly emphasizes that the gospel has been revealed by God and received by us. It is both a *paradosis* (a tradition to be preserved) and a *paratheke* (a deposit to be guarded). We did not invent it, and we have no liberty to edit it or tamper with it. The second ('total fluidity') rightly emphasizes that the gospel must be contextualized, that is to say, related appropriately to each particular person or situation. Otherwise it will be perceived as irrelevant.

Somehow, then, we have to learn to combine these two proper concerns. We have to wrestle with the dialectic between the ancient word and the modern world, between what has been given and what has been left open, between content and context, Scripture and culture, revelation and contextualization. We need more fidelity to Scripture and more sensitivity to people. Not one without the other, but both.

THE CHURCH MUST BE ITSELF: ITS LIFE
The church is supposed to be God's new society, the living embodiment of the gospel, a sign of the kingdom of God, a demonstration of what human community looks like when it comes under his gracious rule.

In other words, God's purpose is that the good news of Jesus Christ is set forth visually as well as verbally, or in the language of the primates' definition, that it be made known 'by word and deed'. Every educator knows how much easier it is for human beings to learn through what they see and experience than through what they hear. Or rather, word and deed, hearing and seeing belong essentially together. This is certainly so in evangelism. People have to see with their own eyes that the gospel we preach has transformed us. As John Poulton put it, 'Christians ... need to look like what they are talking about. It is *people* who communicate primarily, not words or ideas ... What communicates now is basically personal authenticity'.[9] Conversely, if our life contradicts our message, our evangelism will lack all credibility. Indeed, the greatest hindrance to evangelism is lack of integrity in the evangelist.

No text has helped me to understand the implications of this for the life of the local church more than 1 John 4:12: 'No-one has ever seen God, but if we love one another, God lives in us and his love is made complete in us.' God is invisible. Nobody has ever seen him. All that human beings have ever seen of him is glimpses of his glory, of the outshining of his being.

The church is supposed to be God's new society.

Now the invisibility of God is a great problem for faith. It was for the Jews in the Old Testament. Their heathen neighbours laughed at them for actually worshipping an invisible God. 'You say you believe in Yahweh?' they taunted them. 'Where is he? Come to our temples, and we will show you our gods. They have ears and eyes, hands and feet, and mouths and noses too. But where is your God? We can't see him. Ha, ha, ha!' The Jews found this ridicule hard to bear. Hence the complaint of psalmist and prophet, 'Why do the nations say, "Where is their God?"'.[10] Of course Israel had its own apologetic. The idols of the heathen were nothing, only the work of human hands. True, they had mouths, but they could not speak, ears but could not hear, noses but could not smell, hands but could not feel, and feet but could not walk.[11] Yahweh, on the other hand, although (being spirit) he had no mouth, had spoken; although he had no ears, he listened to Israel's prayers; and although he had no hands, he had both created the universe and redeemed his people by his mighty power. At the same time, the people of God longed that he would make himself known to the nations, so that they might see him and believe in him.

The same problem of an unseen God challenges us today, especially people who have been brought up on the scientific method. They are taught to examine everything by their five senses. Anything which is not amenable to empirical investigation they are told to suspect and even reject. So could it ever be reasonable to believe in an invisible God? 'Let us only see him', they say, 'and we will believe.'

How, then, has God solved the problem of his own invisibility? First, he has revealed himself visibly in the world he has made (Romans 1:19–20), for both the heavens and the earth declare his glory (Psalm 19:1–6; Isaiah 6:3). Secondly and supremely, he has revealed himself by sending his Son into the world. 'No-one has ever seen God; the only Son, who is in the bosom of the Father, he has made him known' (John 1:18, RSV). Consequently Jesus could say, 'anyone who has seen me has seen the Father' (John 14:9), and Paul could describe him as 'the [visible] image of the invisible God' (Colossians 1:15).

To this people tend to reply: 'That is truly wonderful, but it happened nearly 2,000 years ago. Is there not a third way in which the invisible God makes himself visible *today*?' Yes, there is. 'No-one has ever seen God' (1 John 4:12). John begins this verse in his first letter with the identical sentence which he has used in the prologue to his Gospel (John 1:18). But now he concludes the sentence differently. In the Gospel he wrote that 'the only Son ... has made him known'. In the letter he writes that 'if we love one another, God lives in us and his love is made complete in us'. Because of John's deliberate repetition of the same statement, this can only mean one thing. The invisible God, who once made himself visible in Christ, now makes himself visible in Christians, *if we love one another.*

God is love in his essential being, and has revealed his love in the gift of his Son to live and die for us. Now he calls us to be a community of love, loving each other in the intimacy of his family – especially across the barriers of age and sex, race and rank – and loving the world in its alienation, hunger, poverty and pain. It is through the quality of our loving that God makes himself visible today.

God calls us to be a community of love.

We cannot proclaim the gospel of God's love with any degree of integrity if we do not exhibit it in our love for others. Perhaps nothing is so damaging to the cause of Christ as a church which is either torn apart by jealousy, rivalry, slander and malice, or preoccupied with its own selfish concerns. Such churches urgently need to be radically renewed in love. As one of the group reports of the 1978

Lambeth Conference put it, 'mission without renewal is hypocrisy'. It is only if we love one another that the world will believe that Jesus is the Christ and that we are his disciples (John 13:35; 17:21).

Here, then, are the four main prerequisites for evangelism through the local church. First, the church must understand itself (theologically), grasping its double identity. Secondly, it must organize itself (structurally), developing a mission strategy which reflects its double identity. Thirdly, it must express itself (verbally), articulating its gospel in a way which is both faithful to Scripture and relevant to the contemporary world. And fourthly, it must be itself (morally and spiritually), becoming so completely transformed into a community of love that through it the invisible God again makes himself visible to the world.

Chapter 4

MINISTRY:
THE TWELVE AND
THE SEVEN

Most churches have some kind of leadership, pastorate or ministry, although they differ in their understanding of it. Yet the Acts of the Apostles throws light on God's purpose for church leaders, especially in chapters 6 (the appointment of the Seven) and 20 (Paul's exhortation to the elders of the Ephesian church).

In the early chapters of Acts Luke does two things. On the one hand he describes the birth and growth of the body of Christ on the Day of Pentecost. On the other he outlines the strategy of Satan, who sought to smother the infant church. One might almost say that, if the chief actor in Acts 1 and 2 was the Holy Spirit, the chief actor in Acts 3 to 6 was that evil spirit called Satan.

True, the devil is mentioned by name only once. This is in Acts 5:3, where Peter asked Ananias how it was that Satan had filled his heart to lie to the Holy Spirit. To outward appearances one man had told a lie to another man. But Peter had the discernment to see beneath the surface. He saw the evil spirit lying to the Holy Spirit. Indeed, Satan had 'filled' Ananias' heart to do so. It was a diabolical parody of Peter being 'filled with the Holy Spirit' (4:8). Our topic, then, is the threefold strategy of Satan.

His first and crudest tactic was physical violence or persecution. He tried to crush the church by force. His second and more subtle tactic was moral compromise: having failed to destroy the church from the outside, he tried to corrupt it from the inside through the deceit of Ananias and Sapphira. His third and subtlest tactic was social distraction: he tried to deflect the apostles from their priority tasks of preaching and prayer. If he had succeeded, and the apostles had given up preaching, an untaught church would have been exposed to every wind of false doctrine.

So these were the devil's chief weapons: persecution, corruption and distraction. Now I do not claim any close personal familiarity with the devil. But what I do know is that he is utterly unscrupulous and entirely lacking in imagination. He has changed neither his strategy nor his tactics. He is still in the same old rut. So a study of his campaign against the early church should alert us. It will leave us no excuse if we are taken by surprise. For my purpose in this chapter, we will concentrate on the third tactic. The story is told in Acts 6:1–7.

AN EVERY-MEMBER MINISTRY

It was a time of exciting church growth (verse 1): 'The number of the disciples was increasing.' But at the same time a serious quarrel broke out between the Grecian Jews (whose language and culture were Greek) and the Hebraic Jews (whose language and culture were Hebrew). The former complained against the latter that their widows were being neglected in the daily distribution of food. At first, it seems that the apostles were trying to tackle the problem themselves. They knew from the Old Testament that God was committed to the care of widows, for 'he defends the cause of the fatherless and the widow' (Deuteronomy 10:18). But the apostles were in danger of becoming preoccupied with administration and of neglecting the ministry of the word.

Faced with these problems, the apostles did a wise thing. They did not impose a solution. Instead they called a church meeting, seeking the wisdom of the whole body. 'It would not be right', they said, 'for us to neglect the ministry of the word of God in order to wait on tables' (verse 2). There is no hint that the apostles regarded social ministry as in any way inferior to pastoral ministry, or beneath their dignity as apostles. It was entirely a question of calling. The apostles had no liberty to be deflected from *their* God-given tasks.

So the apostles made a suggestion, namely that the church should choose seven of their number who were known to be 'full of the Spirit and wisdom', meaning perhaps 'spiritually and practically minded'. Then the apostles would delegate the care of the widows to them, the Twelve to the Seven, while they would concentrate on preaching and prayer. For without prayer it would be unlikely that the seeds sown by the Spirit would be fruitful (verses 3–4).

The church saw the point and agreed. They chose seven men, including Stephen and Philip, whose names all sound Greek, surely to reassure the Grecian Jews who had lodged the original complaint. The church then presented the seven to the apostles, who both prayed for them and laid their hands on them, thus commissioning and authorizing them to exercise their new responsibility (verses 5–6).

> *'Everybody cannot do everything.'*

A vital principle is embedded in this incident, which the church urgently needs to re-learn in every generation, namely that 'everybody cannot do everything'. Indeed, everybody is not called to do everything. Or let me express this principle in three positive statements:

1. God calls all his people to ministry (*diakonia*).
2. God calls different people to different ministries.
3. God expects those called to the ministry of the word to concentrate on their calling and on no account to allow themselves to be distracted by social administration.

It is obviously deliberate that the work of the Twelve and the work of the Seven are both called *diakonia* ('ministry'). The Twelve were called to the *diakonia* of the word (verse 4) or to pastoral ministry, while the Seven were called to the *diakonia* of tables (verse 2) or to social ministry. Neither ministry is inferior to the other. On the contrary, both are Christian ministries (ways of serving God). Both require Spirit-filled people to exercise them. And both can be full-time Christian ministries. The only difference between them is that they are different! The ministry of tables is social ministry, while the ministry of the word is pastoral ministry.

We do a great disservice to the church whenever we refer to the pastorate as 'the' ministry. For if we use the definite article, we give the impression that we think the pastorate is the only ministry there is. I repented of this decades ago, and invite my readers to join me in penitence today. If somebody says in my presence nowadays that so and so is

All Christians are called to ministry.

'going into the ministry', I try to look innocent and respond 'Oh really? Which ministry do you mean?'. To this my interlocutor usually replies 'the pastoral ministry' – to which I reply 'Why did you not say so?'

The truth is that *diakonia* is a generic word for ministry or service. It lacks specificity until we add an adjective – pastoral, social, evangelistic, missionary, medical, legal, educational, administrative, and many more. For example, in Romans 13:4 magistrates and other officials of the state are called *diakonoi Theou*, servants of God, the very expression which could be applied to pastors and other servants of the church.

Let me now sum up the principle which is illustrated in this passage. It is that all Christians are called to ministry (*diakonia*). Because we are followers of him who said he had come not to be served but to serve (Mark 10:45), it is inconceivable that we should spend our lives in any other way than ministry or service. But there is a wide diversity of gifts, callings and ministries, and we have to discover our gifts and help others to discover theirs.

As a direct result of the apostles' delegating the administration to the Seven, and their concentrating on their calling, we read: 'So the word of God spread' and 'the number of disciples . . . increased rapidly' (verse 7). It is only logical that the word cannot spread when the ministry of the word is neglected.

There is a particular application of this principle to the local church. Indeed, it is vital for the health of the local church that pastors and people learn this lesson. True, pastors are not apostles. For the apostles formulated the gospel, whereas pastors are called to expound what the apostles have bequeathed to the church. So it is a real ministry of the word to which pastors dedicate their lives. Yet too often they get distracted and even overwhelmed by administration.

Sometimes it is the pastors' fault, for they want to keep all the reins of leadership in their own hands and refuse to delegate. But sometimes it is the people's fault, for they want their pastor to be a general factotum. 'We pay him', they may say, 'so let him get on with it!' In either case the consequence is disastrous. The standards of preaching decline, and the lay people have little opportunity to exercise their gifts, since the pastor usurps them. So the church falls sick. What is needed is a basic biblical recognition that God calls different people to different ministries. Then the people will ensure that the pastor is set free from unnecessary administration, and pastors will ensure that the people are free to exercise their gifts. It is through this reciprocal liberation that the church will flourish.

I may just add that what Luke describes in Acts, the apostle Paul confirms in his letters. Writing about the *charismata* (spiritual gifts), he emphasizes that there is a wide variety of them (wider than the twelve listed in 1 Corinthians), and that they are intended for the common good, even to build up the body of Christ. Luke and Paul both teach what is sometimes called 'the every-member ministry of the body of Christ'.

> *God calls different people to different ministries.*

THE PASTORAL MINISTRY

We turn now from this every-member ministry, which is shared by all, to the pastoral ministry which is given to some, especially the leadership team.

There is much uncertainty today about the role of the church's leaders. What are 'clergy', if we use this word? Are they priests or pastors, preachers, presbyters, prophets or psychotherapists? Are they educators, facilitators, administrators, managers or social workers? Different answers are given to these questions. In fact the church has oscillated between two opposite unbiblical extremes, namely clericalism (putting them on a pedestal) and anti-clericalism (knocking them off again). Now that churches have recovered the every-member ministry of the local church, people are asking whether clergy are not redundant.

Against this background of uncertainty we turn with relief to Scripture, and in particular to Paul's valedictory address at Miletus to the elders of the Ephesian church (Acts 20:17–38), in which he reflects on his labours among them. We note immediately two characteristics of the oversight of the local church which Paul assumes.

Christian oversight is pastoral oversight.

First, Christian oversight is *pastoral* oversight. The Greek verb in verse 28 (*poimaino*) means to do the work of a shepherd or to tend a flock, especially by feeding it. So pastors are called essentially to a teaching ministry. Whether we are preaching to a congregation, training a group or counselling individuals, ours is a pastoral ministry, a ministry of the word. But how do shepherds feed their sheep? The answer is that they don't. To be sure, if a lamb is sick, a shepherd may bottle-feed it. But usually he leads his sheep into good pastures where they feed themselves.

Secondly, Christian oversight is *plural* oversight. In Miletus the apostle sent for the 'elders' (plural) of the

Ephesian church. There is no biblical warrant for the so-called one-man band, in which a single pastor, like a single musician, plays all the instruments. On the contrary, from the first missionary journey onwards Paul and Barnabas 'appointed elders for them in each church' (Acts 14:23), and later Paul instructed Titus to 'appoint elders in every town' (Titus 1:5). We need, therefore, to recover the concept of the pastoral team in the leadership of the local church. It might consist of full-time and part-time pastors, salaried and voluntary, ordained and lay, younger and older.

Tentatively I would add to this list 'men and women'. The question of women's ministry continues to divide Christian people. Although it is too complex an issue to unravel in a single paragraph, Christians who look to Scripture for their guidance are agreed on certain fundamental truths. Men and women are equal bearers of the divine image and of the earthly dominion (Genesis 1:27), and equal beneficiaries of God's grace in Christ (1 Peter 3:7; Galatians 3:26–28). Thus we are equal before God by both creation and redemption. But we are also complementary to one another (Genesis 2:18–25), and in this complementarity God has given men a certain 'headship' (1 Corinthians 11:3; Ephesians 5:22). How then can equality and complementarity be reconciled? In particular, how can women teach men without infringing

There is no biblical warrant for the so-called one-man band.

masculine headship? Perhaps by remembering that 'headship' means responsibility rather than authority (Ephesians
5:25–30); that what Paul forbids is not so much an office as
an attitude (pride); that what is regarded as inappropriate in
the behaviour and ministry of women varies from culture to
culture; and finally, that the team ministry should be the
norm, in which all members, including women, contribute
their particular gifts to the common good.

Remembering, then, that the leadership of the local
church should be both pastoral and plural, we are ready to
note how Paul in his speech develops the pastoral metaphor.
First, he describes himself and the elders as shepherds.
Secondly, he warns them of the rise of false teachers, whom
he characterizes as wolves. And thirdly he affirms the value of
the people who are God's sheep.

THE EXAMPLE OF THE APOSTLE
(THE SHEPHERD)

In Acts 20:18–27 Paul reminds the elders of his example
while in Ephesus. He is able to say that he has no regrets
about his ministry among them. In particular there had been
a degree of thoroughness about his ministry which was quite
extraordinary, and which left his conscience clear. It had
three aspects.

First, Paul had been thorough in his teaching. He calls
his message 'the gospel of God's grace' (verse 24) and 'the
kingdom' (verse 25). He had also taught them 'repentance
towards God and faith in our Lord Jesus Christ' (verse 21,
NAB). Here are some of the great themes of the gospel –
grace and faith, divine rule and human commitment. In

addition he twice says that he did not shrink from his teaching responsibility, or hesitate to declare both anything profitable to them and the whole plan and purpose of God.

Secondly, Paul had been thorough in his outreach. His goal had been not only to teach the whole purpose of God but also to reach the whole population of Ephesus. He wanted to teach everything to everybody! In consequence his ministry embraced both Jews and Gentiles, both residents and visitors. He spent three months in the synagogue evangelizing Jews and more than two years in the hall of Tyrannus, 'so that all the residents of Asia', that is, of the Roman province of Asia, of which Ephesus was the capital, '. . . heard the word of the Lord' (Acts 19:10, RSV).

Paul's thoroughness remains a challenge to us today.

Thirdly, Paul had been thorough in his methods. He threw himself heart and soul into his ministry. He taught people both publicly (in the synagogue and Tyrannus' hall) and privately ('from house to house'). He also continued day and night. So the apostle had been absolutely indefatigable. Nothing could stop him, not even the fears and trials he experienced. Indeed, he did not consider his life to be of value, since he was quite ready to lay it down, to die as a martyr in the service of the gospel. His ambition was to complete the task which the Lord Jesus had given him, and he had no ulterior motives.

Such was the pastoral thoroughness of the apostle's three years in Ephesus. He omitted no part of God's revealed message. He neglected no segment of the local community. He left no method untried to reach the city. On the contrary, he shared all possible truth with all possible people by all possible means. He taught the whole gospel to the whole city with his whole heart. In consequence he could make this solemn claim, echoing Ezekiel's calling as a faithful watchman: 'I declare to you today that I am innocent of the blood of all men' (verse 26).[1]

Paul's example must have been an unfailing inspiration to the Ephesian elders, and his thoroughness remains a challenge to us today.

THE INVASION OF FALSE TEACHERS
(THE WOLVES)

So far, in the pastoral metaphor which Paul is developing, he has focused on the shepherd and the sheep. Now (verses 28–31) he introduces his hearers to the wolves. It is because savage wolves were going to come in and not spare the flock that the Ephesian elders must be diligent in teaching the truth. Their care of the sheep must be all the more conscientious because of the danger from the wolves.

Now wolves were in the ancient Middle East (and still are in some northern territories) the chief enemy of sheep. Wolves hunt both singly and in packs, and sheep are defenceless against them. Shepherds cannot afford to relax their vigilance. Nor can Christian pastors today.

Paul explains what he means. 'Even from your own number men will arise and will distort the truth in order to draw away disciples after them' (verse 30). And the apostle's prophecy came true, as we see when we read his two later letters to Timothy and Christ's letter to the Ephesian church in Revelation 2. Jesus himself had warned of false prophets. He described them as wearing sheep's clothing, while inwardly they were ferocious wolves (Matthew 7:15).

Therefore, Paul warned the Ephesian elders, 'be on your guard!' Good shepherds (like those in the fields near Bethlehem) must keep watch over their flock by day and night. Just so, good pastors are concerned to guard their people against false teachers. We see, then, that a double task is given to the shepherds of Christ's flock. First, they are to feed the sheep; second, they are to rout the wolves. That is, they are both to teach the truth and to combat error. Paul later tells

A double task is given to the shepherds of Christ's flock.

Titus that candidates for the presbyterate must hold firmly to the teaching of the apostles, so that they may both give instruction in sound teaching and refute those who oppose it (Titus 1:9).

This emphasis on the need to speak against false teaching is very unpopular today. It is frequently said that we must always be positive in our teaching, never negative. But those who say this have either not read the New Testament or, having read it, disagree with it. For our Lord Jesus and his apostles both refuted error themselves and urged us to do the same. I sometimes wonder if the neglect of this necessary ministry is not a major cause of contemporary theological confusion. Theological controversy is always distasteful to sensitive Christian spirits. Woe to us if we enjoy it! But we cannot conscientiously avoid it. If we say and do nothing about obvious false teaching, or if we turn round and flee, we will justly earn the pejorative name 'hireling' or 'hired servant' who cares nothing for the sheep.

Are we to abandon Christ's flock defenceless against the wolves, sheep without a shepherd? Must we say of the church what God said through Ezekiel about Israel: 'So they were scattered, because there was no shepherd and they became food for all the wild beasts' (Ezekiel 34:5). No! It is our plain duty to protect God's flock from error and to establish it in the truth.

THE VALUE OF THE PEOPLE (THE SHEEP)

After the example of the shepherd and the danger of the wolves, Paul turns to the value of the sheep.

> Keep watch over yourselves and all the flock of which the Holy Spirit has made you overseers. Be shepherds of the church of God, which he bought with his own blood (Acts 20:28).

Implicit in verse 28 is the truth that the pastoral oversight of the church belongs to God. He is the supreme overseer of his own people. Indeed each of the three persons of the Trinity has a share in this oversight.

First, the church is God's church. It is not certain whether we should read 'the church of God' (as in NAB and NIV) or 'the church of the Lord' (as in RSV and NEB). In either case the church is God's church; it belongs ultimately to God the Father.

Secondly, it is not certain whether we should read that God purchased it 'with his own blood' (NIV) or 'with the blood of his own' (as in RSV and NEB), meaning 'of his only Son'. In either case the church has been bought with the blood of Christ.

Thirdly, over this church (which belongs to God and has been bought by Christ) it is the Holy Spirit who appoints the overseers. So the oversight is his too, or he could not delegate it.

This is a splendid Trinitarian truth about the church, namely that it belongs to God the Father, has been redeemed by the blood of Christ his Son, and has overseers appointed by God the Holy Spirit.

> *It is not our church; it is God's.*

This fact should humble us. Although we may be privileged to be church leaders, yet it is not our church; it is God's. We have no proprietary rights over it. It may be appropriate for kings and queens to refer to 'my people', but I doubt if it is ever appropriate for pastors to refer to 'my church'. When the Corinthians developed their personality cult and said 'I belong to Paul' or 'I belong to Peter', Paul contradicted them and deliberately reversed their claim. 'All things are yours', he wrote, 'whether Paul or Apollos or Peter' (1 Corinthians 3:21–22). In other words, 'you do not belong to us, we rather belong to you'. To be consistent, therefore, we should refer to *God's* church which we have been called to serve.

This truth should not only humble but also inspire us, and especially motivate us to the loving care of God's people. We need this incentive, for sheep are not at all the clean and cuddly creatures they look from a distance. On the contrary, they are dirty and subject to nasty pests. They need to be regularly dipped in strong chemicals to rid them of lice, ticks and worms. They are also unintelligent and obstinate. I hesitate to apply the metaphor too literally, or describe the people of God as 'dirty, lousy and stupid'! But some church members can be a great trial to their pastors, and *vice versa*. So how shall we persevere in loving the unlovable? Only, I think, by remembering how precious they are. They are so valuable that the three persons of the Trinity are together involved in caring for them. I find it very challenging, when trying to help a difficult person, to say under my breath: 'How precious you are in God's sight! God the Father loves you. Christ died for you. The Holy Spirit has appointed me your pastor. As the three persons of the Trinity are committed to your welfare, it is a privilege for me to serve you.'

Richard Baxter's great book *The Reformed Pastor* (1656) is an exposition of Acts 20:28. Here is a quotation from it:

Oh then, let us hear these arguments of Christ, whenever we feel ourselves grow dull and careless: Did I die for them, and will you not look after them? Were they worth my blood, and are they not worth your labour? Did I come down from heaven to earth, to seek and to save that which was lost, and will you not go to the next door or street or village to seek them? How small is your labour and condescension as to mine! I debased myself to this, but it is your honour to be so employed. Have I done and suffered so much for their salvation; and was I willing to make you a co-worker with me, and will you refuse what little lies on your hands?[2]

Chapter 5

FELLOWSHIP:
THE IMPLICATIONS
OF *KOINONIA*

There is a constant tendency for the meaning of words to be distorted, and for their currency to be devalued, so that words which once throbbed with life are now dead or dying. This is the case with the word 'fellowship'. It is an over-worked and undervalued term. In common usage it means little more than a genial friendliness, a superficial mateyness, what Australian Methodists call a PSA (Pleasant Sunday Afternoon) or a good gossipy get-together over a nice cup of tea.

Yet strong forces are at work toward its recovery: biblical, historical and practical.

To begin with, we have good *biblical* warrant for asserting that it is not good for man to be alone (Genesis 2:18) – an affirmation which Calvin at least saw had a wider reference

than to marriage. Aloneness is not the will of God either in
ordinary life or in the Christian life. People need fellowship
(which we shall still for the moment leave undefined), and it
is God's will that they should have it.

But this basic, biblically recognized need is not completely met by Sunday churchgoing, or even the larger
midweek meetings of the church. There is always something
unnatural and subhuman about large crowds. They tend to
be aggregations rather than congregations – aggregations of
unrelated persons. The larger they become, the less the
individuals who compose them know and care about each
other. Indeed, crowds can actually perpetuate aloneness,
instead of curing it. There is a need, therefore, for large
congregations to be divided into smaller groups, such as
one imagines the house-churches were in New Testament
days.[1] The value of the small group is that it can become
a community of related persons; and in it the benefit of
personal relatedness cannot be missed, nor its challenge
evaded.

This is true of the human family. Our growth into
maturity, according to the purpose of God, takes place in
the context of a family group. It is the complex pattern of
relationships between parents, children, brothers and sisters
which, more than anything else, governs our development
into adult stature. It is the only child and the one-parent
family who often suffer, although even in their case there are
usually relatives, neighbours and friends. Similarly, it is lone
members of the congregation who hold themselves aloof
from a more intimate Christian fellowship, who are likely to
stunt or damage their spiritual progress.

I do not think it is an exaggeration to say, therefore, that small groups, Christian family or fellowship groups, are indispensable for our growth into spiritual maturity. The preservation of solitary Christianity is possible for church-goers who sit sadly isolated in a pew or hide behind a pillar, even if they attend a so-called midweek 'fellowship' where large numbers again gather. Their baptism has made them members of the visible community. By their church attendance they become outwardly conforming members. But still they may not truly belong either to Christ or to the people of Christ.

Small groups are indispensable for our growth into spiritual maturity.

Turning from a biblical to a *historical* argument for small groups, many famous movements of the Spirit of God have either begun or expressed themselves in the intimacy of such fellowship. This was certainly true of the English Reformation, whose roots can be traced to the group of scholars who met in the White Horse Inn in Cambridge to study Erasmus' Greek Testament. It is also true of Methodism, whether one thinks of the original Holy Club in Oxford or of the class meetings of the developed Society. Reference could also be made to the Praying Societies of Scotland and to the fellowship meetings of the East African revival. It is from such small and unpretentious beginnings that great movements have sprung up and spread.

The third argument is *pastoral*. In every church of any size, if it has clergy, they tend to concentrate on nurturing the new convert, visiting the sick, interviewing those to be baptized, confirmed or married, comforting the bereaved, counselling those who ask for help and training workers for witness. But they cannot hope to see or visit all the members of their congregation regularly, at least if it is at all sizeable. Nor indeed should they. The pastoral oversight of the congregation, as we have seen, does not belong exclusively to the ordained ministry.

Moreover, the Bible indicates that each of us is our brother's keeper. It even hints that in one sense every Christian may be regarded as a bishop, because a certain *episcope* ('oversight') is entrusted to every member of the congregation. 'See to it,' we are told in Hebrews 12:15, where the verb is *episkopountes*, 'that no one fails to obtain the grace of God' (RSV). If this is so, it is in fellowship groups that the ideal can become a reality, for in these the minister delegates some *episcope* or pastoral oversight to the lay leaders, and all learn to care for each.

> *In one sense every Christian may be regarded as a bishop.*

This is what John Wesley found. On 25 April 1742 he recorded in his Journal:

I appointed several earnest and sensible men to meet me, to whom I showed the great difficulty I had long found of knowing the people who desired to be under my care. After much discourse, they all agreed there could be no better way to come to a sure, thorough knowledge of each person than to divide them into classes, like those at Bristol, under the inspection of those in whom I could most confide. This was the origin of our classes at London, for which I can never sufficiently praise God, the unspeakable usefulness of the institution having ever since been more and more manifest.[2]

And Dr R. W. Dale commented on this procedure:

Methodism made one striking and original contribution to the institutions of the church, in the Class-meeting. Never, so far as I know, in any church had there been so near an approach to the ideal of pastoral oversight as the Class-meeting, in its perfect form, provides.[3]

Certainly the house-church or home-group movement has been steadily gathering momentum in many parts of the world. In most cases it has no articulated biblical, historical or pastoral rationale. It seems to be largely spontaneous, a genuine movement of the Holy Spirit. If it needs to be explained in terms of human experience, it is probably to be understood as a protest against the dehumanizing processes of secular society and the superficial formalism of much church life. There is a widespread hunger for a life which is genuinely human and absolutely real.

But these images fall far short of what the New Testament calls *koinonia*. We need to rescue it from its caricatures and recover its New Testament authenticity.

At the heart of *koinonia* is the adjective *koinos*, meaning 'common', so that *koinonos* is a 'partner' and the verb *koinoneo* is to 'share'. In particular, *koinonia* bears witness to three things we hold in common. First, it expresses what we *share in* together (our common inheritance); secondly, what we *share out* together (our common service), and thirdly, what we *share with* each other (our mutual responsibility).

OUR COMMON INHERITANCE

In common usage fellowship describes something *subjective*, the experience of warmth and security in each other's presence, as in 'We had good fellowship together'. But in biblical usage *koinonia* is not a subjective feeling at all, but an *objective* fact, expressing what we share in together.

> ## Koinonia
> ## *is an*
> ## objective *fact.*

So Paul could write 'you share in God's grace with me' (Philippians 1:7); John could write '... that you may have fellowship with us, and our fellowship is with the Father and his, Son Jesus Christ' (1 John 1:3); while Paul added 'the fellowship of the Holy Spirit' (2 Corinthians 13:14). Thus authentic fellowship is Trinitarian fellowship. It bears witness to our common share in the grace of God, Father, Son and Holy Spirit.

Is this not what makes us one? We come from different countries, cultures and churches. We have different temperaments, gifts and interests. And yet we have this in common:

the same God as our Heavenly Father; the same Jesus Christ as our Saviour and Lord; and the same Holy Spirit as our indwelling Comforter.

It is our common participation (our *koinonia*) in God (Father, Son and Spirit) which unites us. And this is most vividly expressed in the Lord's Supper or Eucharist. For 'is not the cup of thanksgiving for which we give thanks a participation in the blood of Christ? And is not the bread that we break a participation in the body of Christ?' (1 Corinthians 10:16).

OUR COMMON SERVICE

Koinonia also expresses not only what we have received together, but what we give out together; not only our common inheritance, but also our common service. As we saw in chapter 1, the early Christians 'devoted themselves ... to the fellowship' (Acts 2:42). This is the first use of *koinonia* in the New Testament canon. It does not occur in the Gospels. Indeed it could not, for there was no *koinonia* before the Holy Spirit came.

We are to share not only our material wealth but also our spiritual wealth.

It is clear from Acts 2:44 that Luke is thinking of the common life which the early Christians enjoyed, for *koinonia* is the word Paul used of the collection which he was organizing, and *koinonikos* means generous.

Although only a minority of Christians is called to total voluntary poverty, we are certainly to love one another and to care for our poverty-stricken brothers and sisters. But *koinonia* challenges us to share not only our material wealth but also our spiritual wealth, that is, our knowledge of the gospel. Thus Paul could write 'I thank God ... for your partnership in the gospel from the first day until now' (Philippians 1:5). And it is not far fetched to see Andrew, Peter, James and John as an illustration of this. They were *koinonoi* (partners) in their little fishing business on Lake Galilee. Now Jesus calls them to be partners in fishing for human beings, and catching them for the kingdom of God. Yet there is a strange reluctance among us to engage in personal evangelism. We sometimes sing 'Oh for a thousand tongues to sing my dear Redeemer's praise'. But it is a useless wish. For one thing we will never have a thousand tongues. For another, if we had them, we would not know what to do with them when the one tongue we have is often silent.

OUR MUTUAL RESPONSIBILITY

In the first two aspects of *koinonia*, we are all facing the same way, although in one or other of two directions. But in the third aspect of *koinonia*, when we concentrate on what we share with each other, we are not facing in the same direction. We are rather gathered in a circle facing each other.

Put another way, in this third aspect, we are neither all recipients, nor are we all givers, but we are a partnership in giving and receiving, as Paul says to the Philippians, since he had shared the gospel with them and they had shared a gift with him (Philippians 1:5; 4:15).

Similarly, Paul saw the collection he was organizing from the Greek churches for the Judean churches as a symbol of Gentile-Jewish solidarity in the body of Christ. For since the Gentiles had come to share in the Jews' spiritual blessings, it was appropriate that the Gentiles should share in their material blessings (Romans 15:27). Philippians 4:15 would have been an admirable text for MRI (Mutual Responsibility and Interdependence), which was the programme commended at the Anglican Congress in Toronto in 1963.

Another example may be found in Romans 1, where Paul says that he longs to visit them, partly to impart a spiritual gift to strengthen them, and partly that they might be mutually encouraged by each other's faith, both theirs and his (Romans 1:11–12).

To love each other has very practical consequences.

It is in this connection that we need to consider the many 'one another' words in the New Testament. They describe the reciprocity of Christian fellowship. The commonest example is the command to reciprocal love. Jesus said 'A new command I give you: Love one another. As I have loved you, so you must love one another. By this all people will know that you are my disciples, if you love one another' (John 13:34–35).

Not that this command is romantic or idealistic. To love each other has very practical consequences, both negative and positive. Negatively, if we love each other, we will not stand in judgment on each other, or speak evil against each other. We will not bite or devour each other (as if we were wild beasts). And we will not provoke or envy or lie to each other.

Positively, if we love each other, we will be kind and compassionate to each other, forbear and forgive each other, submit to each other and build each other up, practise hospitality to each other ungrudgingly, encourage each other, admonish and comfort each other, pray for each other and bear each other's burdens.

SOME PRACTICAL ILLUSTRATIONS

One of the most encouraging features of the world Christian scene today has been the recovery of small groups. Many historical movements have begun in the intimacy of small groups. I have already mentioned the beginnings of English Reformation in Cambridge, and the Methodist Revival in Oxford. In my own day, the East African Revival began in the 1930s and has continued with fellowship meetings. Today there is a worldwide proliferation of cell groups, home groups or house churches.

In London we call them fellowship groups because we are anxious that they will exhibit the riches of New Testament *koinonia*. Fellowship groups express what we share in together as we pray and feed on Christ in his word. They express what we share out together. They are encouraged to be outward-looking, to look for opportunities of service, such as inviting local people to evangelistic evenings, visiting the sick and elderly people in their neighbourhood, volunteering to cater for church events and interceding for the world and the church.

Fellowship groups also share with each other. Every time they meet, an opportunity is given to members to share their joys or sorrows, doubts and fears and needs. Of this third type of fellowship John Wesley wrote in his *Plain Account of the People called Methodists*:

> It can scarce be conceived what advantages have been reaped from this little prudential regulation. Many now happily experienced that Christian fellowship of which they had not so much as an idea before. They began to 'bear one another's burdens' and naturally to 'care for one another' ... And 'speaking the truth in love, they grew up into him in all things who is the Head, even Christ'.[4]

Thus fellowship group leaders become mini-pastors, and the pastoral oversight of the congregation is decentralized and shared.

Fellowship groups are composed of human beings, and all human beings differ from one another. We have no desire, therefore, to stereotype a group's programme or development. Nevertheless we believe that true Christian *koinonia* involves the rich and comprehensive sharing which I have tried to unfold. And therefore we constantly keep before our eyes the threefold biblical ideal. We are anxious that the groups will not become unbalanced and degenerate into being merely Bible reading groups, prayer groups, study groups or action groups. We want the fellowship groups to be true to their name, expressing the fullness of *koinonia*. So we keep asking ourselves: are we growing in Christian maturity together? Are we serving the Lord, the church or the world together? Are we increasing in love and care for one another?

Then we may say with confidence and joy, 'we had good fellowship together'.

Chapter 6

PREACHING:
FIVE PARADOXES

The contemporary world is decidedly unfriendly towards preaching. Words have largely been eclipsed by images, and the book by the screen. So preaching is regarded as an outmoded form of communication, what someone has called 'an echo from an abandoned past'. Who wants to listen to sermons nowadays? People are drugged by television, hostile to authority and suspicious of words.

In consequence, some preachers lose their morale and give up. Either they lack the heart to keep going, or they transmogrify the sermon into a sermonette or a little homily or something equally unsatisfactory. My task in this chapter, however, is to try to persuade preachers to persevere, because the life of the church depends on it. If, as Jesus said, quoting Deuteronomy, human beings live by the word of God (Matthew 4:4), it is equally true of churches. Churches live, grow and flourish by God's word, but they languish and perish without it.

I invite you, then, to consider that authentic Christian preaching has a number of indispensable characteristics which appear at first sight to contradict each other, but actually complement each other in the tension of a paradox.

BIBLICAL AND CONTEMPORARY

First, authentic Christian preaching is *both biblical and contemporary*. It is an exposition of Scripture which is related to the world in which we live. Bishop Stephen Neill expressed it well:

> *All Christian preaching is biblical preaching.*

Preaching is like weaving. There are the two factors of the warp and the woof. There is the fixed unalterable element, which for us is the Word of God, and there is the variable element, which enables the weaver to change and vary the pattern at his will. For us that variable element is the constantly changing pattern of people and of situations.[1]

I hope we are agreed that all Christian preaching is biblical preaching. We do not occupy the pulpit in order to preach ourselves, broadcast our theories or ventilate our opinions. No! Our understanding of preaching is that it is essentially an exposition of the word of God. In that sense all

Christian preaching is 'expository' preaching – not in the narrow sense of that term (a running commentary on a long passage), but in the broad sense (it opens up the biblical text). For we are trustees of God's revelation and are determined above all else to be faithful in our stewardship.

As Dr Donald Coggan, a former Archbishop of Canterbury, wrote:

> The Christian preacher has a boundary set for him. When he enters the pulpit he is not an entirely free man . . . He is not at liberty to invent or choose his message; it has been committed to him, and it is for him to declare, expound and commend it to his hearers . . . [2]

At the same time, authentic Christian preaching is contemporary. It resonates with the modern world. It wrestles with the realities of our hearers' situation. In our resolve to be biblical, we refuse to lapse into irrelevance. Instead we seek to relate the ancient text to the modern context.

I like to imagine this as a picture, of a flat territory deeply cut by a canyon or ravine. On one side is the biblical world, on the other side the modern world, while between the two there is a deep gulf, two thousand years of changing culture.

Evangelical believers live in the biblical world. That is where we feel comfortable. We believe, love and read the Bible. We are essentially biblical people. But we are not so comfortable in the modern world. We feel threatened by it. So how should I draw our preaching on this picture? It all comes out of the Bible. We would not dream of preaching from anywhere else. But then it goes up in the air and never quite lands on the other side. We are biblical, but not contemporary.

Liberal preachers, on the other hand, make the opposite mistake. They live in the modern world and do not feel threatened by it. They read modern poetry, philosophy, psychology, science and novels. They are moving with the moving times. But their situation is that they have largely jettisoned the biblical revelation. So when I draw their preaching on the picture, it all lands in contemporary reality. But where it comes from, heaven alone knows; it does not come out of the Bible. They are contemporary but not biblical.

Authentic Christian preaching is a bridge-building operation.

This simple picture illustrates one of the major tragedies in the church today. Evangelicals are biblical but not contemporary, while liberals are contemporary but not biblical. Comparatively few are building bridges. But authentic Christian preaching is a bridge-building operation. It relates the text to the context in such a way as to be both faithful to the biblical text and sensitive to the modern context. We must not sacrifice either to the other.

In order to build bridges which are solid, we have to study on both sides of the canyon. It goes without saying that we must study Scripture until we are really familiar with it. But we must also study the world in which we live. Nothing has helped me do this more than belonging to a reading group which began in 1972. We met every few weeks, having read an agreed non-Christian book, to discuss its challenge to our Christian world-view. I call this 'double listening', listening to the word of God and listening to the voices of the modern world, its cries of anger, pain and despair.

AUTHORITATIVE AND TENTATIVE

The twentieth century was an epoch of doubt. True, it began with a decade of Edwardian triumphalism. While Edward VII was on the British throne, everything seemed stable and fixed, even immovable. But the sinking of the *Titanic* in April 1912 was an omen of worse disasters to come. For the social stability, which characterized the Edwardian era, was shattered by two World Wars and their aftermath. All the old landmarks (symbols of stability) were destroyed. Now, in the twenty-first century, people are floundering in the swamps of relativism and uncertainty. Even the church seems as blushingly insecure as an adolescent teenager. Many preachers conceive their task as sharing their doubts instead of their faith. For the parading of personal doubt belongs to the very essence of postmodernism.

So on the one hand it is vital to recover the voice of authority in the pulpit. Bishop J. C. Ryle of Liverpool (1880–1900) complained that 'a vast quantity of modern preaching is so foggy and hazy and dim and indistinct and hesitating and timid and cautious and fenced with doubts, that the preacher does not seem to know what he believes himself.'[3]

Not that we should ever presume to use the formula 'Thus says the Lord'. That was the language of the biblical prophets, who were organs of divine revelation, but preachers are not prophets in that sense. Our formula is rather, 'the Bible says', provided that we have done our hermeneutical homework and have been conscientious in applying proper principles to the text. Then we shall be able to preach with courage and conviction.

On the other hand, alongside authoritative preaching, it is often right to be tentative. For God has not revealed everything; he has deliberately kept some things secret. 'The secret things belong to the LORD our God, but the things that are revealed belong to us and to our children for ever' (Deuteronomy 29:29). This is why Christians combine elements of dogmatism and agnosticism. We should be dogmatic about those things which have been plainly revealed, and agnostic about those things which have been kept secret. Our troubles arise when our dogmatism trespasses into the secret things, and our agnosticism into the revealed things.

Moreover, even what God has revealed is not always plain. True, we believe in the perspicuity of Scripture (that it has a transparent or see-through quality), but the Reformers were alluding to the central message of salvation by grace alone through faith alone. That is as plain as day. Even the simplest people can understand it. But the Reformers did not claim that everything was equally plain. How could they when the apostle Peter confessed that there were some things in Paul's letters which he found hard to understand (2 Peter 3:15–16). If one apostle could not always understand another apostle, it would hardly be modest for us to claim that we can!

So I would like to see in the pulpit, alongside the authority which belongs to God's infallible revelation, the due humility and diffidence which belong to its fallible human interpreters. Commenting on Romans 10:14–17, Calvin wrote: 'I shall state my own view freely, but each must form his own judgment.'

Besides, if we serve everything up on a plate (pre-cooked and ready to eat), we condemn our congregation to perpetual immaturity. Is this not why Jesus forbade his disciples to call anybody their father or teacher on earth (Matthew 23:8–10)? That is, we must not adopt towards anybody on earth, or require anybody to adopt towards us, the dependent relationship of children to their parents or disciples to their guru. There are to be no gurus in the Christian community – only pastors (shepherds).

All preaching should lead people into the Scriptures.

But shepherds do not feed their sheep. Instead, as we saw earlier, they lead them to good, green pasture where the sheep feed themselves. Thus all preaching should lead people into the Scriptures and encourage them to browse there for themselves.

It is not easy to strike a balance between the authoritative and the tentative, the dogmatic and the agnostic, the infallible word and its fallible interpreters. But we must struggle to do so. I would like to see among us preachers more confidence in what God has revealed, alongside more reticence before what he has kept secret.

PROPHETIC AND PASTORAL

The next paradox is that between the prophetic and the pastoral. Indeed, not only authentic Christian preaching, but the whole church is called to this double ministry – 'prophetic' in the sense that we bear witness (without fear or favour) to the doctrinal truths and ethical standards which God has plainly revealed; and 'pastoral' in the sense that we deal gently with those who are slow to believe biblical truth and who fail to attain biblical standards.

On the one hand, some preachers have a very faithful prophetic ministry. They show great courage in declaring God's word. They refuse to compromise it even to the smallest degree. They remember that it is false prophets who say 'peace, peace' when there is no peace. So they include warnings of judgment in their message.

But these prophetic witnesses are often pastorally very insensitive. They exhibit little of 'the meekness and gentleness of Christ' (2 Corinthians 10:1). They seem to enjoy seeing the congregation squirm under their lash. They even do what Scripture says the Messiah would never do: they break bruised reeds and snuff out smouldering wicks (Isaiah 42:3; Matthew 12:20). If they are faced with Paul's dilemma 'shall I come to you with a whip, or in love and with a gentle spirit?' (1 Corinthians 4:21), they opt for the whip.

Other preachers excel in pastoral love and care. Their favourite words are 'tolerance' and 'compassion'. They know the frailty and vulnerability of human nature; and they make due allowances for it. They remember that Jesus did not condemn the woman caught in the act of adultery; so they seek to be non-judgmental in their relationships.

But they forget that Jesus also told the adulteress to go and leave her life of sin (John 8:1–11). He also told the Samaritan woman to fetch her husband and so to face her sin. By forgetting the holiness of God's love, and his call to repentance, their prophetic witness is blunted and their trumpet does not give a clear sound.

It is not easy to combine prophetic witness and pastoral care, firmness and gentleness, discipline and compassion. I think it was Chad Walsh, an American Episcopal layman, who first defined preaching as 'disturbing the comfortable and comforting the disturbed'.[4]

GIFTED AND STUDIED

We now face the question: who and what makes a preacher? Does God create preachers? Or do they have a share in the creative process? The answer to these questions must again be 'both'. It is the fourth paradox of preaching.

On the one hand, every authentic preacher has been called, equipped and anointed by God. The very concept of a self-appointed, self-made preacher is grotesque. For preaching is a gift. The five New Testament lists of *charismata* include pastors and teachers, together with the gifts of exhortation and encouragement. It is highly significant that when Paul lists ten conditions of eligibility for the presbyterate, nine of them are moral and spiritual (for example, hospitality and self-control), and only one could be classified as 'professional', namely *didaktikos*, having a gift for teaching (1 Timothy 3:2).

It is a mistake, therefore, to distinguish between 'institutional' and 'charismatic' ministers, as if the former are appointed by the church, and the latter by God. No! The church has no liberty to ordain those whom God has neither called nor gifted. On the contrary, what is ordination? We should agree that it includes at least a public acknowledgment by the church that God has called the candidates, together with a public commissioning of them to exercise the ministry to which God has called them and for which he has gifted them. In particular, a gift for teaching is an indispensable qualification. Without this gift and its accompanying call nobody can be a teacher or preacher.

The very concept of a self-appointed, self-made preacher is grotesque.

On the other hand, the divine call, gift and anointing are not enough. The gift has to be nurtured and developed by those to whom it has been given. So Timothy was exhorted not to neglect his gift, but rather to fan it into flame (1 Timothy 4:14; 2 Timothy 1:6). How to do this he was not told, but presumably it would be by disciplined prayer and study, and by the conscientious exercise of his gift.

One still sometimes meets preachers who are suspicious of the exhortation to study. They think that it is incompatible with the anointing of the Spirit, and that if they were really trusting in the Holy Spirit, study would be superfluous. Some even quote Jesus for support: 'Do not worry about what to say or how to say it. At that time you will be given what to say, for it will not be you speaking, but the Spirit of your Father speaking through you' (Matthew 10:19–20). But the context for this promise is the law court not the church, and the people to whom the promise is made are prisoners in the dock, not preachers in the pulpit!

We have to do the reflecting and the thinking.

A more appropriate text for preachers is 2 Timothy 2:7: 'Reflect on what I am saying, for the Lord will give you insight into all this' (NIV) or 'Think over what I have said, and the Lord will give you full understanding' (NJB). The two parts of this verse need to be kept together. It is indeed God who gives us understanding or insight; but we have to do the reflecting and the thinking.

This need for study or reflection has long been recognized. Calvin wrote that 'no-one will ever be a good minister of the Word of God unless he is first of all a scholar'.[5] Spurgeon had the same conviction: 'He who no longer sows in the study will no more reap in the pulpit'.[6] And here is a longer passage from Bishop Phillips Brooks in his 1877 Yale Lectures:

The preacher's life must be a life of large accumulation ...
Learn to study for the sake of truth, learn to think for the profit
and the joy of thinking. Then your sermons shall be like the
leaping of a fountain, and not like the pumping of a pump.[7]

In our own century Billy Graham has added his voice to
this chorus. Speaking in 1979 to about 600 pastors in
London, he said that if he had his ministry all over again, he
would make two changes. The atmosphere was electric.
What changes would he make? First, he continued, he
would study three times as much as he had done. 'I've
preached too much', he said, 'and studied too little.' Second,
he would pray more. In saying this, he must have had in
mind the two apostolic priorities which we considered in
chapter 4: 'we will give our attention to prayer and the
ministry of the word' (Acts 6:4).

THOUGHTFUL AND PASSIONATE

The third paradox is thoughtful and passionate, by which we
mean that in all authentic preaching the mind and the
emotions are both engaged; clear thinking and deep feeling
are combined.

Some preachers are extremely thoughtful. Their desk is
piled high with commentaries and other books. Their biblical
orthodoxy is impeccable. They not only study, but they bring
the fruits of their study into the pulpit. Each sermon is the
product of painstaking exegesis and application.

But their sermons are also dry as dust and dull as
ditchwater. They would never lean over the pulpit with
tears in their eyes, begging people to be reconciled to God.

There is no feeling in their sermons, no heat, no heart, no passion. They would never provoke a child, as Charles Simeon did, to cry: 'O Mama, what is the gentleman in a passion about?' Yet how can anybody preach the gospel of Christ crucified and not feel moved by it?

Other preachers are all fire and no light. They rant and rave in the pulpit. They work themselves up into a frenzy like the prophets of Baal. Every sermon is one long, fervent, even interminable appeal. But the people are confused as to what they are being urged to do because there has been no exposition before the appeal. It is a safe rule to insist on no appeal without an exposition and no exposition without an appeal. The apostle Paul is a fine example of this combination in 2 Corinthians 5. First came the exposition: 'All this is from God, who reconciled us to himself through Christ' (verse 18). Then came the appeal: 'We implore you on Christ's behalf: Be reconciled to God' (verse 20).

In all authentic preaching the mind and the emotions are both engaged.

One of Richard Baxter's favourite axioms was 'first light, then heat', and C. H. Spurgeon wrote:

> There must be light as well as fire. Some preachers are all light and no fire, while others are all fire and no light. What we want is both fire and light.[8]

Similarly, in his book entitled *Preaching and Preachers* Martyn Lloyd-Jones wrote:

> What is preaching? Logic on fire! Eloquent reason! Are these contradictions? Of course they are not. Reason concerning this truth ought to be mightily eloquent, as you see it in the case of the apostle Paul and others. It is theology on fire. And a theology which does not take fire, I maintain, is a defective theology; or at least the man's understanding of it is defective. Preaching is theology coming through a man who is on fire.[9]

Here then are the five paradoxes of preaching. Authentic Christian preaching is:

both biblical and contemporary
    (relating the ancient text to the modern context);
both authoritative and tentative
    (distinguishing between the infallible word and its
        fallible interpreters);
both prophetic and pastoral
    (combining faithfulness with gentleness);
both gifted and studied
    (necessitating a divine gift and human self-discipline);
both thoughtful and passionate
    (letting the heart burn as Christ opens to us the
        Scriptures).

The devil is the enemy of all balance and moderation. One of his favourite hobbies is to tip Christians off balance. If he cannot get us to deny Christ, he tries to make us distort Christ. Instead, we need to develop 'BBC' (balanced, biblical

Christianity) by combining truths which complement one another and not separating what God has joined. For it is in these unresolved paradoxes that authentic Christian preaching is to be found.

Chapter 7

GIVING:
TEN PRINCIPLES[1]

Christian giving is an extremely important topic on the contemporary church's agenda. Local churches are often preoccupied with financial concerns, and worldwide I doubt if there is a single Christian enterprise which is not hindered and hampered by lack of funds. How then can we think biblically about Christian giving?

It is well known that the apostle Paul organized a collection from the Greek churches of Achaia and Macedonia for the benefit of the impoverished churches of Judea. Indeed, it may seem extraordinary that he should have devoted so much space in his letters to this mundane matter, referring to it in Romans 15, 1 Corinthians 16 and 2 Corinthians 8 – 9. But Paul did not see it as a mundane matter. On the contrary he saw it as relating to the grace of God, the cross of Christ and the unity of the Spirit. In fact, it is very moving to grasp this combination of profound Trinitarian theology and practical common sense.

In 2 Corinthians 8 and 9, the apostle Paul develops ten principles of Christian giving.

SPRINGING FROM THE TRINITY

First, Christian giving is *an expression of the grace of God*.

> And now, brothers, we want you to know about the grace that God has given the Macedonian churches. Out of the most severe trial, their overflowing joy and their extreme poverty welled up in rich generosity. For I testify that they gave as much as they were able, and even beyond their ability. Entirely on their own, they urgently pleaded with us for the privilege of sharing in this service to the saints. And they did not do as we expected, but they gave themselves first to the Lord and then to us in keeping with God's will. So we urged Titus, since he had earlier made a beginning, to bring also to completion this act of grace on your part (2 Corinthians 8:1–6).

Notice that Paul does not begin by referring to the generosity of the churches of Macedonia in northern Greece. He refers instead to the generosity of God, 'the grace that God has given the Macedonian churches'. Grace is another word for generosity. In other words, behind the generosity of Macedonia, Paul saw the generosity of God. Our gracious God is a generous God, and he is at work in his people to make them generous too.

Three tributaries came together in the river of Macedonian generosity, namely their severe trial, their overflowing joy and their extreme poverty. In consequence, the Macedonians gave even beyond their ability, and they pleaded for the privilege of doing so. How easily our comfortable Western culture can deaden our sensitivity to others' needs. The Macedonians had no such comfort, and no such lure of personal satisfaction. Their values were entirely different. They gave themselves first to the Lord, and then to Paul and his fellow workers. What a model for the Corinthians, and for us!

We read next how Paul had urged Titus to complete what he had begun in Corinth, the capital of Achaia, some time before. What had Titus begun? He had been exhorting the Corinthians to give in the same way as the Macedonians.

Our gracious God is a generous God.

This then is where Paul begins – with the grace of God in the Macedonian churches of northern Greece and with the same grace of God in the Achaian churches of southern Greece. Their Christian generosity was an outflow of the generosity of God.

Secondly, *Christian giving can be a* charisma, *that is, a gift of the Spirit.*

> But just as you excel in everything – in faith, in speech, in knowledge, in complete earnestness and in your love for us – see that you also excel in this grace of giving (2 Corinthians 8:7).

The Corinthians already excelled in the spiritual gifts of faith, speech, knowledge, earnestness and love, and now the apostle urges them to excel also 'in this grace of giving'. Similarly in Romans 12:8 Paul includes in another list of *charismata*, 'contributing to the needs of others'. The grace of giving is a spiritual gift.

Many of God's gifts are both generously bestowed in some measure on all believers and given in special measure to some. For example, all Christians are called to share the gospel with others, but some have the gift of an evangelist. All Christians are called to exercise pastoral care for others, but some are called to be pastors. Just so, all Christians are called to be generous, but some are given the particular 'gift of giving'. Those entrusted with significant financial resources have a special responsibility to be good stewards of those resources.

All Christians are called to be generous.

Thirdly, *Christian giving is inspired by the cross of Christ.*

> I am not commanding you, but I want to test the sincerity of your love by comparing it with the earnestness of others. For you know the grace of our Lord Jesus Christ, that though he was rich, yet for your sakes he became poor, so that you through his poverty might become rich (2 Corinthians 8:8–9).

Paul was not commanding the Corinthians to give generously. This is not how he deals with them. Rather he puts the sincerity of their love to the test by comparing them with others and especially (it is implied) with Christ. For they knew 'the grace of our Lord Jesus Christ'.

Let us note this further reference to divine grace. The grace of God is at work in us, and the grace of Christ challenges us to respond in like manner. Let us not rush on, for here is one of the most searching principles Paul describes. Notice the two references to poverty and the two references to wealth. Because of our poverty Christ renounced his riches, so that through his poverty we might become rich. It is not material poverty and wealth which Paul has in mind. No, the 'poverty' of Christ is seen in his incarnation and especially his cross, while the 'wealth' he gives us is salvation with all its rich blessings.

As we give, may we, too, reflect on the cross.

As we give, may we, too, reflect on the cross, and all that was achieved for us through the death of Christ. How meagre are our earthly riches in comparison!

CREATING EQUALITY ACCORDING TO OUR MEANS

Fourthly, *Christian giving is proportionate giving.*

And here is my advice about what is best for you in this matter: Last year you were the first not only to give but also to have the desire to do so. Now finish the work, so that your eager willingness to do it may be matched by your completion of it, according to your means. For if the willingness is there, the gift is acceptable according to what one has, not according to what he does not have (2 Corinthians 8:10–12).

During the previous year the Corinthian Christians had been the first not only in giving but in desiring to give. So now Paul urges them to finish the task they had begun, so that their doing will keep pace with their desiring. This must be according to their means. For Christian giving is proportionate giving. The eager willingness comes first; so long as that is there, the gift is acceptable in proportion to what the giver has.

This expression 'according to your means' might remind us of two similar expressions which occur in Acts. In Acts 11:29 members of the church in Antioch gave to the famine-stricken Judean Christians 'each according to his ability'. In Acts 2 and 4 members of the church in Jerusalem gave 'to each according to his need'.

Does this ring a bell in our memories? In his *Critique of the Gotha Programme* (1875) Marx called for a society which could inscribe on its banners 'from each according to his ability' and 'to each according to his need'. I have often wondered if Marx knew these two verses in Acts and if he deliberately borrowed them. Whatever our politics and economics may be, these are certainly biblical principles to which we should hold fast. Christian giving is proportionate giving.

Of course there are times when we are called to give as the Macedonians gave, out of proportion to their income, as a sacrificial offering in particular circumstances. But the principle here is a foundational one. Christian giving should never be less than proportionate to our income.

Fifth, *Christian giving contributes to equality*.

> Our desire is not that others might be relieved while you are hard pressed, but that there might be equality. At the present time your plenty will supply what they need, so that in turn their plenty will supply what you need. Then there will be equality, as it is written: 'He who gathered much did not have too much, and he who gathered little did not have too little' (2 Corinthians 8:13–15).

Paul's desire, as he goes on to explain, is not that others may be relieved while they are hard pressed, for that would merely reverse the situation, solving one problem by creating another, but rather 'that there might be equality'. At present, Corinthian plenty will supply the needs of others, so that in turn, at a later stage, the plenty of others will supply Corinthian need. 'Then there will be equality.' Paul illustrates the principle from the supply of manna in the desert. God provided enough for everybody. Larger families gathered a lot, but not too much. Smaller families gathered less, but not too little, and they had no lack.

Paul is putting the affluence of some alongside the need of others, and calling for an adjustment, that is, an easing of need by affluence. This was with a view to *isotes*, the Greek word which can mean either 'equality' or 'justice'.

What is this 'equality' for which Paul calls? It has three aspects.

First, it is not egalitarianism. God's purpose is not that everybody receives an identical wage, lives in an identical house, equipped with identical furniture, wears identical clothing and eats identical food – as if we had all been mass-produced in some celestial factory! No. Our doctrine of creation should protect us from any vision of colourless uniformity. For God the Creator has not cloned us. True, we are equal in worth and dignity, equally made in God's image. True, God gives rain and sunshine indiscriminately to both the evil and the good. But God has made us different, and has given his creation a colourful diversity in physique, appearance, temperament, personality and capacities.

Secondly, at least in the contemporary world, it begins with equality of educational opportunity. Christians have always been in the forefront of those urging literacy and education for all. For to educate (*educare*) is literally to lead people out into their fullest created potential, so that they may become everything God intends them to be. For example, equal educational opportunity does not mean that every child is sent to university, but that every child capable of benefiting from a university education will be able to have one. No child should be disadvantaged. It is a question of justice.

Thirdly, equality sees an end to extreme social disparity. Julius Nyerere, former President of Tanzania, said in his Arusha Declaration that he wanted to build a nation in which 'no man is ashamed of his poverty in the light of another's affluence, and no man has to be ashamed of his affluence in the light of another's poverty'.

The same dilemma confronts missionaries. Should they 'go native', becoming in all things like the nationals they work among? Or should they continue to enjoy Western affluence without any modification of their lifestyle? Probably neither. The Willowbank Report on 'Gospel and Culture' (1978) suggests that they should rather develop a standard of living 'which finds it natural to exchange hospitality with others on a basis of reciprocity, without embarrassment'.[2]

In other words, if we are embarrassed either to visit other people in their home, or to invite them into ours, because of the disparity of our economic lifestyles, something is wrong; the inequality is too great, for it has broken the fellowship. There needs to be a measure of equalization in one or other direction, or in both. And Christian giving contributes to this equality.

There needs to be a measure of equalization.

CAREFUL SUPERVISION AND FRIENDLY RIVALRY

The sixth principle is that *Christian giving must be carefully supervised*.

I thank God, who put into the heart of Titus the same concern I have for you. For Titus not only welcomed our appeal, but he is coming to you with much enthusiasm and on his own initiative. And we are sending along with him the brother who is praised by all the churches for his service to the gospel. What is more, he was chosen by the churches to accompany us as we carry the offering, which we administer in order to honour the Lord himself and to show our eagerness to help. We want to avoid any criticism of the way we administer this liberal gift. For we are taking pains to do what is right, not only in the eyes of the Lord but also in the eyes of men.

In addition, we are sending with them our brother who has often proved to us in many ways that he is zealous, and now even more so because of his great confidence in you. As for Titus, he is my partner and fellow-worker among you; as for our brothers, they are representatives of the churches and an honour to Christ. Therefore show these men the proof of your love and the reason for our pride in you, so that the churches can see it (2 Corinthians 8:16–24).

Handling money is a risky business, and Paul is evidently aware of the dangers. He writes 'we want to avoid any criticism of the way we administer this liberal gift', and 'we are taking pains to do what is right, not only in the eyes of the Lord but also in the eyes of men'. He was determined not only to do right, but to be seen to do right.

So what steps did Paul take? First, he did not handle the financial arrangements himself, but put Titus in charge of them and expressed his full confidence in him. Secondly, Paul added that he was sending along with Titus another brother, who was 'praised by all the churches for his service to the gospel'. Thirdly, this second brother had been 'chosen by the churches to accompany' Paul and carry the gift (see also 1 Corinthians 16:3). The people carrying the offering to

Jerusalem had been elected by the churches because of their confidence in them.

It is wise for us now to take similar precautions against possible criticism. It is good for churches to be openly careful about the number of people present when the offering is counted, and for regular reports to be given to church members on the church finances. We need such transparency in church life; it gives confidence to the membership.

For mission agencies it is important to have a board giving wise and experienced oversight of the financial operations, so that money received from supporters can be invested well and pressed effectively into service. On a broader canvas, we can be thankful for the work of auditors, and for the government's oversight of all charitable giving through the Charity Commission, or its equivalent, which regulates both good practice and good reporting.

Handling money is a risky business.

The seventh principle is that *Christian giving can be stimulated by a little friendly competition.*

There is no need for me to write to you about this service to the saints. For I know your eagerness to help, and I have been boasting about it to the Macedonians, telling them that since last year you in Achaia were ready to give; and your enthusiasm has stirred most of them to action. But I am sending the brothers in order that our boasting about you in this matter should not prove hollow, but that you may be ready, as I said you would be. For if any Macedonians come with me and find you unprepared, we – not to say anything about you – would be ashamed of having been so confident. So I thought it necessary to urge the brothers to visit you in advance and finish the arrangements for the generous gift you had promised. Then it will be ready as a generous gift, not as one grudgingly given (2 Corinthians 9:1–5).

Paul had been boasting to the churches of northern Greece (e.g. Philippi) about the eagerness of the churches of southern Greece (e.g. Corinth) to give, and this enthusiasm had stirred the northerners to action. Now Paul is sending the brothers already mentioned to Corinth to ensure that his boasting about the southerners will not prove hollow, and that they will be ready as he had said they would be.

For if some northerners were to come south with Paul and find the southerners unprepared, it would be a huge embarrassment. So Paul sent the brothers in advance, to finish the arrangements for their promised gift. Then they would be ready and their gift would be generous and not grudging. First Paul boasted of southern generosity, so that the northerners will give generously. Now he urges the southerners to give generously, so that the northerners will not be disappointed in them.

It is rather delightful to see how Paul plays off the north and the south against each other to simulate the generosity of both. Competition is a dangerous game to play, especially if it involves publishing the names of donors and the amounts donated. But we can all be stimulated to greater generosity by hearing about the generosity of others.

In some churches the church council or elders are invited ahead of the rest of the congregation to pledge first to a church building project, and the total raised (without individual names) is announced before the church gift day. It can build faith for church members to know that their leaders are truly behind these special giving projects, where much sacrificial giving is needed.

A HARVEST WITH SYMBOLIC SIGNIFICANCE
The eighth principle is that *Christian giving resembles a harvest.*

> Remember this: Whoever sows sparingly will also reap sparingly, and whoever sows generously will also reap generously. Each man should give what he has decided in his heart to give, not reluctantly or under compulsion, for God loves a cheerful giver. And God is able to make all grace abound to you, so that in all things at all times, having all that you need, you will abound in every good work. As it is written: 'He has scattered abroad his gifts to the poor: his righteousness endures forever.' Now he who supplies seed to the sower and bread for food will also supply and increase your store of seed and will enlarge the harvest of your righteousness. You will be made rich in every way so that you can be generous on every occasion... (2 Corinthians 9:6–11a).

Two harvest principles are applied here to Christian giving.

First, we reap what we sow. Whoever sows sparingly reaps sparingly, and whoever sows generously reaps generously. 'Sowing' is an obvious picture of giving. What then can we expect to 'reap'? We should not interpret Paul's point too literally, as if he were saying that the more we give the more we will get. No. Each of us should give 'what he has decided in his heart to give', neither reluctantly, nor under compulsion, but rather ungrudgingly, because 'God loves a cheerful giver'. Let's pause for a moment on that phrase 'what he has decided in his heart to give'. There is a sense here of a settled conviction about how much to give; of a decision reached after careful consideration, and always with joy and cheerfulness.

> *It is rarely necessary to give on the spur of the moment.*

It is good to remind ourselves here of Paul's earlier letter to the Corinthians and his exhortation to systematic giving (1 Corinthians 16:1–3). Everyone should, he said, set aside a sum of money in relation to his income 'on the first day of the week'. Our facility of setting up a bank transfer, for both our church giving and our mission giving, would be very much in keeping with this. We're reminded again here of the importance of 'deciding'. It is rarely necessary to give on the spur of the moment. How much better to take time and seek that settled conviction.

If we give in this spirit, what will happen? What harvest can we expect to reap? The answer is twofold: 'God is able to make all grace abound to you' so that 'in all things' (not necessarily in material things) you may have all you need; and you will 'abound in every good work' because your

opportunities for further service will increase. As the psalmist says, the consequence of giving to the poor is to have a
righteousness which endures for ever (Psalm 112:9).

Secondly, what we reap has a double purpose. It is both
for eating and for further sowing. The God of the harvest is
concerned not only to alleviate our present hunger, but to
make provision for the future. So he supplies both 'bread for
food' (immediate consumption) and 'seed to the sower' (to
plant when the next season comes round). In the same way
God will 'supply and increase your store of seed and will
enlarge the harvest of your righteousness'.

These verses are the origin of the concept of 'seed-money',
expecting God to multiply a donor's gift. Paul is not teaching
a 'prosperity gospel', as some have claimed. True, he promises
that 'you will be made rich in every way', but he adds at once
that this is 'so that you can be generous on every occasion' and
so increase your giving. Wealth is with a view to generosity.

The ninth principle is that *Christian giving has symbolic
significance.*

There is more to Christian giving than meets the eye. Paul
is quite clear about this. In the case of the Greek churches,
their giving symbolized their 'confession of the gospel of
Christ' (2 Corinthians 9:13). How is that?

Paul looks beyond the mere transfer of cash to what it
represents. The significance was more than *geographical*
(from Greece to Judea) or *economical* (from the rich to the
poor). It is also *theological* (from Gentile Christians to Jewish
Christians), for it was a deliberate, self-conscious symbol of
Jewish-Gentile solidarity in the body of Christ.

Indeed, this truth (that Jews and Gentiles are admitted to

the body of Christ on the same terms, so that in Christ they are heirs together, members together and sharers together) was the 'mystery' which had been revealed to Paul.[3] This was the essence of his distinctive gospel. It was the truth he lived for, was imprisoned for and died for. It is hinted at here, but elaborated in Romans 15:25–28.

Paul wrote there that the Gentile churches of Greece had been 'pleased' to make a contribution for the impoverished Christians of Judea. 'They were pleased to do it', he repeated. Indeed 'they owe it to them. For if the Gentiles have shared in the Jews' spiritual blessings' (culminating in the coming of the Messiah himself), 'they owe it to the Jews to share with them their material blessings' (Romans 15:27). It was a striking illustration and declaration of Christian fellowship.

Our Christian giving can express our theology.

In similar ways, our Christian giving can express our theology. For example, when we contribute to evangelistic enterprises, we are expressing our confidence that the gospel is God's power for salvation, and that everybody has a right to hear it. When we give to economic development, we express our belief that every man, woman and child bears God's image and should not be obliged to live in dehumanizing circumstances. When we give to the maturing of the church, we acknowledge its centrality in God's purpose and his desire for its maturity.

THE RESULT: THANKSGIVING TO GOD

Finally, *Christian giving promotes thanksgiving to God.*

Four times in the concluding paragraph of these two chapters (2 Corinthians 9:11b–15), Paul states his confidence that the ultimate result of the Corinthians' offering will be to increase thanksgiving and praise to God. This is at the heart of all spiritual giving.

your generosity will result in thanksgiving to God (verse 11)

this service that you perform ... is ... overflowing in many expressions of thanks to God (verse 12)

men will praise God for the obedience that accompanies your confession of the gospel of Christ, and for your generosity (verse 13)

Thanks be to God for his indescribable gift! (verse 15)

Authentic Christian giving leads people not only to thank us, the givers, but to thank God, and to see our gift to them in the light of his indescribable grace, shown supremely in the gift of his Son.

It is truly amazing that so much is involved in this transfer of money. We have the doctrine of the Trinity – the grace of God, the cross of Christ and the unity of the Holy Spirit; and we have the practical wisdom of an apostle of Christ. Spiritual truth and practical wisdom are both at work, side by side.

What an awesome privilege we have in helping others right across the world to give glory to God. Releasing more of the money which he has entrusted to us as stewards will end in this. And to increase thanksgiving to God for the sake of his own glory is surely our highest goal.

I hope that this study of these chapters in 2 Corinthians will help to raise our giving to a higher level, and will persuade us to give more thoughtfully, more systematically and more sacrificially. I for one (speaking to myself first) have already reviewed and raised my giving. I venture to hope that you may do likewise.

Chapter 8

IMPACT:
SALT AND LIGHT

One of the most important questions facing Christians in every age and every place is this: what values and standards are going to dominate our national culture? Most countries today are increasingly pluralistic in both race and religion. That is to say Christianity, Islam, secularism, materialism, ancient religions and modern cults are all competing for the soul of our country. Which is going to win? For Christians this is primarily an evangelistic question. Will Jesus Christ be given the honour which is due to his name? For God has super-exalted him, in order that every knee should bow to him and every tongue confess him 'Lord'.

But it is also a social and cultural question. Will Christians be able to influence their country so that the values and standards of the kingdom of God permeate the whole national culture – its consensus on moral and bioethical issues, its recognition of human rights, its respect for the sanctity of human life (including that of the unborn, the handicapped and the senile), its concern for the homeless, the unemployed and people trapped in the cycle of poverty, its attitude to dissidents, its stewardship of the environment, its treatment of criminals, and the whole way of life of its citizens? All this and more is 'the national culture'.

There can surely be no doubt that our Lord Jesus Christ wants *his* values and standards to prevail. For he loves righteousness and hates evil (Psalm 45:7) wherever they are found. So he sends his people out into the world both to preach the gospel and make disciples, and to sweeten the whole community and make it more pleasing to God, more just, more participatory, more free.

Will Christians be able to influence their country?

These are certainly mega-claims. Can they be justified? Do they have a biblical basis? I think they do, and that we may find them in Mathew 5:13–16:

> You are the salt of the earth, but if the salt loses its saltiness, how can it be made salty again? It is no longer good for anything, except to be thrown out and trampled by men. You are the light of the world. A city on a hill cannot be hidden. Neither do people light a lamp and put it under a bowl. Instead they put it on its stand, and it gives light to everyone in the

house. In the same way, let your light shine before men, that they may see your good deeds and praise your Father in heaven.

We are all familiar with salt and light. They are two of the commonest household necessities. They are found in virtually every home in every culture throughout the world. Certainly everybody used them in the Palestine of Jesus's day. He will have known them from boyhood, and must often have watched his mother use salt in the kitchen. In those days before refrigeration salt was used not so much for flavouring as for preservative and antiseptic purposes. So Mary will have put salt on the fish and have rubbed it into the meat, or left them to soak in salty water. And she will have lit the oil lamps when the sun went down.

Now these are the images or models which Jesus chose to indicate the impact he intended his followers to exert in the world. What did he mean? What is it legitimate for us to deduce from his choice of metaphors? My answer is that by the models of salt and light Jesus was teaching four truths about his church collectively and his followers individually. It is up to my readers to decide whether these deductions are legitimate or not.

THE TRUTHS OF SALT AND LIGHT

First, *Christians are radically different from non-Christians*, or ought to be. Both images (salt and light) set the two communities in contrast to each other. On the one hand there is the world, which with all its evil and tragedy is like a dark night, whereas on the other hand there is 'you' who are to be the dark world's light. Again, on the one hand there is the world, which is like rotting meat and decaying fish, whereas on the other hand there is 'you' who are to be its salt, hindering social decay. We might have said in our idiom that they are as different as oil from water. But Jesus said we are to be as different as light from darkness and salt from decay.

This is a major theme of the whole Bible, namely that God is calling out a people for himself, whom he intends to be different from the prevailing culture. 'Be holy', he says to them 'for I am holy'. In the Sermon on the Mount Jesus said to his disciples 'do not be like them' (Matthew 6:8), and in Romans Paul wrote, 'Do not conform any longer to the pattern of this world' (Romans 12:2). It is the call to be radically different.

Jesus said we are to be different.

Secondly, *Christians must permeate non-Christian society.* Although spiritually and morally distinct, we are not to be socially segregated. On the contrary, 'let your light shine'. That is, let it penetrate the darkness. Don't light your lamp, Jesus continued, and put it under your bed or in some dark cupboard. Instead, put your lamp on a lamp stand and let its light shine out. In other words, let the good news of Jesus Christ, who is the light of the world, spread throughout society by both your words and your deeds.

Similarly, the salt must penetrate the meat. A lamp does no good if it is stowed in a cupboard, and salt does no good if it stays in a salt-cellar. The light must shine into the darkness, and the salt must soak into the meat. Both models illustrate the process of penetration and call us to permeate society. Yet too many of us hide away in our dark little cupboards and stay snug in our elegant little ecclesiastical salt-cellars.

The Fabian Society was founded in 1884 by George Bernard Shaw, Sidney Webb and others. Its avowed purpose was to make Britain socialist – not by a Bolshevik revolution, nor by political intrigue and conspiracy, but by a policy of infiltration. In particular, they sought to permeate the Conservative and Liberal parties (at that time there was no Labour Party) with Socialist ideas. Later H. G. Wells quarrelled with the founding fathers and pronounced their infiltration policy a failure.

> *Too many of us hide away in our dark little cupboards.*

They had permeated English society, he said, with their reputed socialism about as much (or as little) as a mouse may be said to permeate a cat. In other words they had been swallowed by society instead of permeating it. The same, alas!, could be said of many of us Christians today.

One way to permeate secular culture for Christ is through our daily work. I was brought up as a young man to believe in a pyramid of vocations. At its apex was the cross-cultural missionary. He was our hero, she our heroine. If we were not as zealous for Christ as that, we would stay at home and become a pastor. If that were beyond us, we would go for one of the great professions (law, education or medicine), whereas if we went into politics or the media we were surely not far from backsliding.

But I have long since blown up this pyramid. Don't misunderstand me. It is a wonderful thing to be a missionary or a pastor *if God calls one to it*. But it is equally wonderful to be a doctor, teacher or lawyer if that is one's calling. And we urgently need more Christians, if called, to go into politics and the media and live there for Christ.

Thirdly, *Christians can influence and change non-Christian society*. We may now be entering more controversial territory, but let us continue to consider the implications of the salt and light metaphors.

Salt and light are both effective commodities. They change the environment into which they are introduced. Thus, when salt is introduced into meat or fish, something happens; bacterial decay is hindered. Again, when the light is switched on, something happens; the darkness is dispelled. Further, it may be argued that salt and light have complementary effects. The influence of salt is negative; it hinders bacterial decay. The influence of light is positive; it illumines the darkness. Just so, the influence of Christians on society is intended by Jesus to be both negative (checking the spread of evil) and positive (promoting the spread of truth and goodness, and especially of the gospel).

So why don't we Christians have a more wholesome effect on society? We look at deteriorating trends around us. We see social injustice, racial conflict, violence in the streets, corruption in high places, sexual promiscuity, and the scourge of HIV-Aids. Who is to blame? Our habit is to blame everybody except ourselves. But let me put it in a different way.

If the house is dark at night, there is no sense in blaming the house for its darkness. That is what happens when the sun goes down. The question to ask is: where is the light?

Again, if the meat goes bad and becomes inedible, there is no sense in blaming the meat for its decay. That is what happens when the bacteria are left free to breed. The question to ask is: where is the salt?

Similarly, if society becomes corrupt (like a dark night or stinking fish), there is no sense in blaming society for its corruption. That is what happens when human evil is unchecked and unrestrained. The question to ask is: where is the church? Where is the salt and light of Jesus?

We must accept the role which Jesus has assigned to us.

It is hypocritical to raise our eyebrows and shrug our shoulders as if it were not our responsibility. Jesus told us to be salt and light to society. If therefore darkness and rottenness abound, it is to a large measure our fault, and we must accept much of the blame.

We must also accept, with fresh determination, the role which Jesus has assigned to us, namely to be salt and light to society. It is not only individuals who can be changed; societies also can be changed. Of course we cannot perfect society, but we can improve it. Christians are not utopians.

Not until Christ comes in glory will there be a perfect society of peace and justice. But meanwhile history is full of examples of social improvements – rising standards of health and hygiene, greater availability of literacy and education, the emancipation of women, better conditions in mines, factories and prisons, and the abolition of slavery and of the slave trade.

We cannot claim that all these improvements are due entirely to Christian influence. But we can claim that (through his followers) Jesus Christ has had an enormous influence for good.

WEAPONS FOR SOCIAL CHANGE

Professor Kenneth Scott Latourette of Yale University wrote a seven-volume *History of the Expansion of Christianity*. Some of his concluding words are as follows:

> No life ever lived on this planet has been so influential in the affairs of men [as that of Christ] . . . From that brief life and its apparent frustration has flowed a more powerful force for the triumphal waging of man's long battle than any other ever known by the human race.[1]

But how does social change take place? I want to suggest that Christians have six weapons in their armoury.

First, there is *prayer*. I beg you not to dismiss this as a pious platitude. Christians believe that God hears and answers prayer. So the apostle commands us (as a priority) to pray for national leaders, so that 'we may live peaceful and quiet lives' (1 Timothy 2:1–2). Yet when I visit some churches there is almost no intercession. I sometimes wonder if the slow progress towards world peace and world evangelization is due to the prayerlessness of the people of God. For example, when President Marcos of the Philippines was toppled in 1986, Filipino Christians attributed it not so much to 'people power' as to 'prayer power'. We should take the task of public intercession more seriously than we commonly do. If local churches were to bow down before God every Sunday for ten or twenty or even thirty minutes, what might God be free to do?

Christian social responsibility depends on socially responsible Christians.

Secondly, there is *evangelism*, which has an indispensable part to play in relation to social change. For Christian social responsibility depends on socially responsible Christians, and socially responsible Christians are the fruit of evangelism. It is when the Holy Spirit changes us that we begin to develop a social conscience and gain the vision and courage to change our society.

When John V. Taylor (late Bishop of Winchester) reviewed Geoffrey Moorhouse's book *Calcutta*, he wrote about the apparent hopelessness of that city's problems:

But invariably what tips the balance of despair to faith is the person who rises above the situation. Moorhouse's book is full

of such persons (William Carey, Mother Teresa and others) . . .
They are neither trapped in the city, nor escaped from it. They
have transcended the situation. Salvation is not the same as
solution; it precedes it and makes it a possibility . . . Personal
salvation – salvation in first gear – is still the way in. It is the key
to unlock the door of determinism . . . [2]

The third weapon in our armoury is *example*. Human
beings are imitative by nature. So there is great power in
example. A single Christian who takes an uncompromising
stand for righteousness, encourages others to follow. One
Christian home can influence a whole neighbourhood. A
dedicated Christian group (in school or college, hospital,
office or factory) can change its atmosphere and its accepted
values. And the local church is meant by God to be 'a sign of
the kingdom', a model of what human community looks
like when it comes under the rule of God, an attractive
alternative society.

Our fourth weapon is *argument*. In the end unjust social
structures can be changed only by legislation. Legislation
cannot make bad people good, but it can reduce the level of
evil in society and so make it more pleasing to God.

Martin Luther King understood this difference. 'Morality
cannot be legislated,' he wrote, 'but behaviour can be
regulated. Judicial decrees may not change the heart, but
they can restrict the heartless.'[3]

Again he wrote:

Government action is not the whole answer to the present
crisis, but it is an important partial answer . . . The law cannot

make an employer love me, but it can keep him from refusing to hire me because of the colour of my skin.[4]

In a democracy legislation depends on consent, and consent depends on consensus (that is, public opinion), and consensus depends on argument, indeed on getting into the public debate and winning the argument.

We need to pray that God will raise up more ethical thinkers, who will not just climb Mount Sinai and declaim the Ten Commandments, but will argue that God's standards are best. Just as we need theological apologists, who will argue the truth of God's gospel, so we need ethical apologists who will argue the goodness of God's law.

All of us are called to be responsible citizens.

The fifth weapon in our Christian armoury is *action*, that is, socio-political action. But, it may be responded, should not Christians steer clear of politics? The answer is that it depends what we mean by 'politics'? The narrow definition is that politics is the science of government, the framing of laws which embody the beliefs and values of society. The broad definition, however, since *polis* means the city, is living together in community. In the narrow sense politics is for the politicians. It is their vocation to develop policies and programmes for legislative change. In the broad sense, however, politics is meant for everybody, since Jesus sends us all into the world to serve, and all of us are called to be responsible citizens, to exercise our democratic rights, to vote and seek to influence other people's votes, to speak up and write on current issues, and to engage in public, peaceful protest and witness, and in these ways to be salt and light to society.

The sixth and last weapon in our armoury is *suffering*, that is, a willingness to suffer for what we believe in. Suffering is a test of our authenticity. Both evangelism and social action are costly activities. For both the gospel of Christ and the moral standards of Christ are unpopular. They challenge our selfishness. So those who defend God's law and God's gospel are bound to suffer opposition.

Suffering is a test of our authenticity.

We have considered six weapons in our Christian arsenal. Each is powerful on its own; together they are truly formidable. They indicate that the church should make a strong impact on society. Robert N. Bellah, retired sociology professor at the University of California at Berkeley, made this remarkable statement:

I think we should not underestimate the significance of the small group of people who have a new vision of a just and gentle world ... The quality of a culture may be changed when 2% of its people have a new vision.[5]

CHRISTIAN DISTINCTIVES

Reverting to the significance of salt and light, we affirm fourthly that *Christians must retain their Christian distinctness.* Salt must retain its saltiness. Otherwise it becomes useless; you cannot even throw it on the compost heap. In the same way, light must retain its brightness. Otherwise it will never dispel the darkness. Just so, we Christians, if we are to influence society, must not only permeate it but also refuse to conform to it. We must retain our Christian convictions, and especially the values, standards and lifestyle of the kingdom of God. Otherwise we will have no effect and make no impact.

What, then, are our Christian distinctives? What is the salt and the light which we are told to be? The rest of the Sermon on the Mount tells us. For in it Jesus describes the citizens of the kingdom, the members of his new community.

First, *Christ calls us to a greater righteousness.* 'For I tell you that unless your righteousness surpasses that of the Pharisees and the teachers of the law, you will certainly not enter the kingdom of heaven' (Matthew 5:20). The disciples must have been dumbfounded when they heard these words, for the scribes and Pharisees were the most righteous people on earth. They calculated that the law contained 248 commands and 365 prohibitions, making 613 regulations altogether, and they claimed to have kept the lot! Now Jesus says that unless his disciples are more righteous than the most righteous people, they will never even enter the kingdom! Has the Master lost his reason? No, Christian righteousness is greater than Pharisaic righteousness because it is deeper. It is a righteousness of the heart. It therefore necessitates a new heart by a new birth.

Secondly, *Christ calls us to a wider love*. Here is the last of the six antitheses which he expressed: 'You have heard that it was said "love your neighbour and hate your enemy". But I tell you: "Love your enemies and pray for those who persecute you"' (Matthew 5:43–44). 'Love your neighbour and hate your enemy' is a scandalous misquotation of the Old Testament. The law said 'Love your neighbour' (Leviticus 19:18). It was the Pharisees who indulged in a culpable casuistry, saying to themselves, 'My neighbour is my co-religionist. If, therefore, it is only my neighbour that I am to love, the law itself gives me permission to hate my enemy.'

Christ calls us to a wider love.

Jesus responded by insisting that, in the vocabulary of God, our neighbour includes our enemy. If, then, we love our enemy, we will be authentic children of our Heavenly Father. For he gives sunshine and rain to all people indiscriminately. His love is all-embracing; ours must be too.

Thirdly, *Christ calls us to a nobler ambition*. All human beings are ambitious. Ambition is the desire to succeed. In the words of Jesus ambition is what we 'seek', what we set our hearts on as the supreme good to which we devote out lives. In the end, Jesus teaches, there are only two options. It is either ourselves and our own material comfort or we seek first God's kingdom and righteousness (Matthew 6:31–34). To become absorbed with ourselves and our bodies (food, drink and clothing) is a hopelessly inadequate preoccupation for the children of God. In the Lord's Prayer Jesus has already established what our priorities should be, namely God's name, kingdom and will.

Here then is the call of Christ – to a greater righteousness (a righteousness of the heart), to a wider love (a love of the enemy), and to a nobler ambition (God's rule and God's righteousness). Only then will our salt retain its saltiness, and our light its brightness, so that we will be salt and light to the world.

We need in particular to repent of our pessimism. Christians have no business to be pessimists. Faith and pessimism are incompatible. To be sure, we are not starry-eyed idealists; we are down-to-earth realists. We know

Christ calls us to a nobler ambition.

well that sin is ingrained in human nature and in human society. We are not expecting to build utopia. But we also know that the gospel has transforming power, and that Christ has commissioned us to be effective salt and light in the world.

So let us offer ourselves to God as agents of change. Let's not excuse ourselves by developing a minority complex!

This is the optimism of Edward Everett Hale (1822–1909), an American Unitarian minister and writer, who lived and worked in Boston, Massachusetts, and inspired many by his story *Ten Times One is Ten*:[6]

> I'm only one,
>   but I am one.
> I can't do everything,
>   but I can do something.
> What I can do,
>   I ought to do.
> And what I ought to do,
>   by the grace of God
>   I will do.

And if that is true of an individual Christian, how much greater an impact should the church be able to make!

CONCLUSION: LOOKING FOR TIMOTHYS IN THE TWENTY-FIRST CENTURY

I began this book with a Preface which acknowledged that many people today are looking for a 'fresh expression' of the church. My concern has been that in this legitimate process of exploration they will not forget, let alone abandon, certain biblical and history-proven marks of a living church. I have attempted to expound eight of these.

And now I bring the main body of this book to a conclusion with a personal appeal to church leaders, whether clergy or laity. Like Timothy, you are called to guard the gospel and to conduct yourselves appropriately in God's household, 'which is the church of the living God, the pillar and foundation of the truth' (1 Timothy 3:15).

Now that I am in the ninth decade of my life, I often find myself looking into the future and longing that God will raise up a new generation of Timothys. In this conclusion I venture to address my appeal to you, praying that you may know God's grace in your life and ministry.

I guess that you find Timothy, as I do, a very congenial

character. I have a very soft spot in my heart for Timothy, for he seems to have been one of us in all our human frailty. Timothy was no stained glass saint. A halo would not have fitted comfortably on his head.

For one thing, he was still comparatively young when Paul wrote him his first letter. Probably by now he was in his thirties, but he was still inexperienced for the heavy responsibilities which were being laid on him. He was also temperamentally shy, for Paul needed to tell the Corinthians to put him at ease when he visited them (1 Corinthians 16:10). Then thirdly he had a recurrent gastric problem, for which Paul prescribed a little alcoholic medicine.

Timothy was called to be different from the prevailing culture.

So this was Timothy – young, shy and frail. These are three disabilities which are often found in Christian people today. But they endear him to us. He needed the power of Christ in his weakness, as we do. Let us heed the challenge which Paul addressed to Timothy near the end of his first letter:

But you, man of God, flee from all this, and pursue righteousness, godliness, faith, love, endurance and gentleness. Fight the good fight of the faith. Take hold of the eternal life to which you were called when you made your good confession in the presence of many witnesses (1 Timothy 6:11–12).

We notice that Paul's exhortation begins with the two words 'but you'. It is an expression which occurs several times in Paul's letters to Timothy and which indicates that Timothy was called to be different from the prevailing culture around him. He was not to drift with the stream, or to bend before the pressures of public opinion, like a reed shaken by the wind. Instead, he must stand firmly (as we must) like a rock in a mountain stream.

The reason was that he was a 'man of God'. In the Old Testament this honorific title was reserved for leaders like Moses, David, Elijah and other prophets. But in the New Testament it appears to apply to every mature Christian who is 'thoroughly equipped for every good work' (2 Timothy 3:17). False teachers were men and women of the world, but the men and women of God derive their values and their standards from God himself.

A THREEFOLD APPEAL

The apostle now develops a threefold appeal to Timothy – ethical, doctrinal, and experiential.

First comes *the ethical appeal.* Timothy is to 'flee from all this', literally 'from all these things', referring in the context to covetousness and all the evils associated with it. Included in these, although mentioned only later, will have been 'the evil desires of youth' (2 Timothy 2:22) such as immorality, selfish ambition, indiscipline and impetuosity. Instead, Timothy is given six beautiful qualities to pursue – righteousness and godliness, faith and love, endurance and gentleness. More simply, Timothy is to run away from evil and to run after goodness.

Now we human beings are great runners. We run from danger, which threatens us. But we also run away from issues and responsibilities which we dare not face. Paul seems to be saying to us that instead we should be running away from evil.

Positively, we tend to run after whatever attracts us. We run after pleasure, success, fame, wealth and power. Instead, Paul seems to be saying, how about running after goodness in its many and varied forms?

There is no passivity in the attainment of holiness. We do not just sit there and do nothing, letting God do it all. The apostle gives Timothy no secret to learn, no technique to master, and no formula to recite. We just have to run for our lives, running away from evil and running after righteousness. The apostle calls us to be good runners.

We should be running away from evil.

Secondly, there is *the doctrinal appeal*. 'Fight the good fight of the faith.' In all three Pastoral Letters (addressed to Timothy and Titus) we are informed that there is such a thing as revealed truth. It is given different names, such as the faith, the teaching, the tradition, the truth, and the deposit. This is of course the teaching of the apostle Paul and of his fellow apostles. This is the true apostolic succession, namely the continuity of doctrine handed down from the apostles, bequeathed to us, and safeguarded by the church in every generation. We are to defend it, proclaim it, and teach it with all faithfulness.

Just as good and evil are contrasted with one another in 1 Timothy 6:11, so truth and error are contrasted in verse 20. In other words, in both the ethical and the doctrinal appeal which Paul addresses to Timothy – and so to us – we have complementary responsibilities. Ethically we are to run away from evil and to run after goodness. Doctrinally we are to turn away from error and fight for the truth.

And it is a fight to which we are called. Nobody enjoys fighting, except perhaps those who are pugnacious by temperament. Fighting is distasteful to every sensitive spirit. There is something sick about enjoying controversy. Nevertheless, the apostle calls it 'the *good* fight' (verse 12), since the glory of God and the well-being of the church are both involved. Even the gentleness which we are to pursue according to the previous verse is not to stop us from fighting for the truth. We must not shirk this unpleasant duty.

It is a fight to which we are called.

Thirdly, there is *the experiential appeal*. 'Take hold of the eternal life to which you were called.' The important thing about eternal life is not its duration but its quality. It is the life of the new age. Jesus himself defined it. Speaking to his Father, he said: 'Now this is eternal life: that they may know you, the only true God, and Jesus Christ whom you have sent' (John 17:3). It is in this personal relationship with God that eternal life is to be found.

Timothy had been called to this. Presumably there had been a private call, but also a public one when he had made his 'good confession in the presence of many witnesses' at his baptism. So Paul says to him, in effect, that he possessed eternal life because it had been given to him when he believed and was baptized. So now he was to lay hold of it.

WHERE ARE THE TIMOTHYS?

It was surely strange, however, that a Christian leader of Timothy's maturity should need to be exhorted to lay hold of what he already possessed. Had he not been a Christian for many years? Yes, he had. Had he not received eternal life as a free gift many years ago? Yes, he had. Then why did Paul tell him to lay hold of what was already in his possession?

The answer to these questions is that it is possible to possess something without embracing or enjoying it. The Greek verb *epilambano* contains a hint of violence. It is used, for example, of the soldiers when they laid hold of Simon of Cyrene and compelled him to carry the cross instead of Jesus. It is also used of the mob in Jerusalem when they dragged Paul outside the Temple area. So Paul's appeal to Timothy was to seize hold of the eternal life which was already his own. He was to make it increasingly his. He was to enjoy it, to experience it to the full.

This difference between possession and enjoyment is well illustrated in the story of Louis Delcourt. He was a young French soldier during the First World War who overstayed his leave and, fearing disgrace, he decided to desert. He persuaded his mother to lock him up in the attic of their home and there she hid him and fed him for twenty-one years. But in August 1937 his mother died. There was no chance now of his retaining his incognito and remaining in hiding. So, pale and haggard, he staggered along to the nearest gendarmerie, where he gave himself up. The gendarme looked at him in utter incredulity and asked him, 'where have you been that you have not heard?' 'Haven't heard what?' asked Louis. 'That a law of amnesty for all deserters was passed years ago.'

It is possible to possess something without embracing or enjoying it.

Louis Delcourt had freedom but did not enjoy it because he did not know that he had it. It is the same with many Christian people today. They have been set free by Jesus Christ. But they are not enjoying their freedom because they do not know that they have it.

We can learn two valuable lessons from Paul's threefold appeal to Timothy.

First, consider the extreme *relevance* to our day of this threefold appeal. The apostle seems to set before us here three absolute goals. There is such a thing as goodness: pursue it. The postmodern mood is unfriendly to all universal absolutes. Yet the apostle says there is such a thing as truth: fight for it. And there is such a thing as life: lay hold of it. May God enable us to make an unabashed commitment to those three absolutes – to what is true, what is good, and what is real.

Consider secondly the *balance* of Paul's threefold appeal. That is to say, it incorporates within itself doctrine, ethics and experience.

Some Christians fight the good fight of the faith. They are great warriors for the truth. But they do not pursue goodness, let alone gentleness.

Others are good and gentle, but they have no comparable concern to fight for the truth.

Yet others neglect both doctrine and ethics, and concentrate on their quest for religious experience.

Why must we always polarize? All three of these are God's purpose for us. Oh, for balanced Christians!

So where are the Timothys of the twenty-first century? They seek to be loyal not only to one or other of these three goals, but to the whole biblical revelation without picking and choosing what they happen to like. They pursue righteousness, they fight the good fight of the faith, and they lay hold of eternal life simultaneously.

THREE HISTORICAL
APPENDICES

An autobiographical sketch

I. *Why I am still a Member of the Church of England*
   (18 October 1966)

II. *I Have a Dream of a Living Church*
    (24 November 1974)

III. *Reflections of an Octogenarian*
     (27 April 2001)

THREE HISTORICAL
APPENDICES

Related in different ways to the living church

AN AUTOBIOGRAPHICAL SKETCH

This brief autobiographical sketch seemed to me to be necessary. It explains how I became so closely attached to All Souls Church. It also introduces the three historical appendices which follow. These record three significant dates in my developing story.

I have had the extraordinary experience of being a member of the same parish church for almost the whole of my life – as a child, as a student, as a newly ordained curate, as Rector and as Rector Emeritus.

I was only a few months old when my parents, my sisters and I moved from Kensington to Harley Street, the so-called 'Doctors' Street' where we made our home and my physician-father had his consulting room for seeing private patients.

My mother took my sister and me to All Souls Church for Sunday morning worship; it was barely 200 yards from our home. At first Arthur Buxton was Rector (1920–36) and then Harold Earnshaw Smith (1936–50). My most vivid memory of Sunday worship was of sitting in the gallery, making paper pellets out of bus tickets, and dropping them onto the fashionable hats of the ladies below. Little did I imagine that some twenty-five years later I would occupy the pulpit as Rector! Such is the redeeming and transforming power of the gospel. Another memory of childhood was that my sister Joy and I were taken on Sunday afternoons to a Sunday School for doctors' children in the Rectory, led by Esmé Buxton, the Rector's wife.

I was at Rugby School when I first knowingly heard the gospel and responded to it. Within a few months, astonished that I had never before heard the good news, I had a growing sense of vocation to share with others what nobody till then had shared with me. And because I had told this to my headmaster, I was exempt from military service as an ordinand.

So I spent the war years at Trinity College, Cambridge, studying first French and German, and then theology. Soon after graduation, on one of his many visits to Cambridge, Harold Earnshaw-Smith invited me after ordination to serve my curacy at All Souls under him. It seemed the most natural thing in the world that I should begin my ordained ministry in the parish in which I had been brought up – though using different ammunition from bus ticket pellets!

I was ordained by the Bishop of London in St Paul's Cathedral on 21 December 1945. The Earnshaw-Smith family befriended me, and I was fortunate enough to have Harold as my mentor, who inducted me into the rudiments of pastoral ministry. There was only one snag: his health. Half way through my first year in the parish, he was taken ill with his first coronary. He was away for several weeks, and even when he returned he was convalescing and able to manage only a little work, so that at least for a while the weight of the parish rested on Gordon Mayo, my fellow-curate, and me. In 1947 Harold Earnshaw-Smith was again taken ill, and for the next two or three years he was back and forth between the parish and convalescence. In early March 1950 he again left London to convalesce on the south coast, and one week later he died in his sleep. I was put in charge of the parish, and four months later to everybody's astonishment (especially mine) I was appointed to succeed him as Rector.

WHY I AM STILL
A MEMBER OF THE
CHURCH OF ENGLAND

(18 October 1966)

On 18 October 1966 the Second National Assembly of Evangelicals opened in the Methodist Central Hall, Westminster, with Dr Martyn Lloyd-Jones as keynote speaker and myself in the chair. The meeting led to a historic confrontation between us, which has rumbled on for forty years. Dr Lloyd-Jones appealed to evangelicals in mixed denominations to leave them, while I felt it right to urge such people not to take any rash action, since the issue was due to be debated the following morning. The incident has been written up in several histories and biographies.[1]

My purpose in referring to this disagreement of long ago is not so much to resurrect a debate as to take the opportunity to respond to people who still ask me whether my position has changed, and if so how.

This historical appendix began its life as my contribution entitled 'I Believe in the Church of England' to Gavin Reid's symposium *Hope for the Church of England?* (Kingsway, 1986). Twenty years later it was picked by Caroline Chartres and reduced for her symposium *Why I Am Still an Anglican* (Continuum, 2006), with some changes.

So do I believe in the Church of England? Yes, I believe in the Church of England. At least, I do and I don't. I do not believe in the Church of England, of course, in the sense that I believe in God – Father, Son and Holy Spirit – as the object of my confidence and worship. Yet I do believe in the Church of England in the sense that I am deeply grateful to be a member and a minister of it, and to be able to remain such with a good conscience. So I will start by sketching four distinctive features of the Church of England, which also constitute four reasons why I belong to it. They apply to some degree to all Anglicans, but relate specifically to the Church of England.

First, the Church of England is *a historical church*. It is, in fact, the church of the English people. It traces its origins back, not to Henry VIII and his matrimonial problems (the notorious 'King's Matter'), but to the first century AD when the Roman legions were colonizing the empire. Merchants followed them, and among these soldiers and tradesmen there must have been followers of Jesus Christ. Both Tertullian and Origen round about the year 200 AD spoke of a church in England. St Alban died as a martyr for Christ, probably during the Decian persecution of 250 AD. At the Synod of Arles in 314 AD there were three British bishops. So the Church of England is the historic church of this country.

Now this historical dimension is important today in a world that is busy cutting adrift from its historical roots. For the living God of the Bible is the God of history, the God of Abraham, Isaac and Jacob, the God of Moses and the prophets, the God of our Lord Jesus Christ and his apostles, and the God of the post-apostolic church. One of the weaknesses of the house-church movement is that it has little sense of history, little sense of continuity with the past.

Secondly, the Church of England is *a confessional church*. We move now from history to theology. According to 1 Timothy 3:15, the church is 'the pillar (*stulos*) and bulwark (*hedraioma*) of the truth'. *Hedraioma* may mean either 'bulwark' or 'foundation'. In either case it holds a building firm, while pillars thrust the building aloft. So the church is called to serve the truth, both holding it firm and holding it high for people to see. The Church of England, therefore, has doctrinal standards and a confession of faith. The Book of Common Prayer and the Thirty-Nine Articles remain the doctrinal basis of the Church of England, in spite of the weakening of the formula of assent and the arrival of the more recent service books. Moreover, these standards affirm the supremacy of Scripture over traditions, the sufficiency of Scripture for salvation, and the justification of sinners by grace alone, in Christ alone, through faith alone. These three doctrines are particularly dear to evangelical believers, and they are plainly affirmed in our Anglican Articles.

It is true that there are a few church leaders who deny some fundamentals of the faith, and this is both a tragedy and a scandal. But the Church of England has never abandoned its confession of faith. It is a confessional church.

Thirdly, the Church of England is *a national church*. It is not a 'state' church like the continental Lutheran churches, but it is an 'established' church (recognized by law and given certain privileges), and – more important – it is a 'national' church because it has a national mission. In ideal and purpose, then, the Church of England is neither a sect, nor a denomination, but the church of the nation, with a responsibility to be the nation's conscience, to serve the nation.

It is perfectly true that in practice this ideal often breaks down. Nevertheless, although adaptations may be necessary the Church of England remains a national church.

Fourthly, the Church of England is *a liturgical church*. It has a Book of Common Prayer, and a Common Worship service book, containing services for public worship. Some say that set services inhibit spontaneity and the freedom of the Spirit. This does not have to be the case. Form and freedom are not necessarily incompatible with one another. Certainly, we welcome the greater flexibility which the new service books have given us. But rightly they have not abandoned a liturgical framework and form.

Why should we value a liturgy? First, there is plenty of biblical warrant for liturgical forms. The New Testament contains many snatches of ancient hymns and credal statements, for Christians took this over from the Old Testament. Secondly, a liturgy enshrines truth and safeguards uniformity of doctrine. Thirdly, it gives a sense of solidarity both with the past and with the rest of the church in the present. Fourthly, it protects the congregation from the worst idiosyncrasies of the clergy. Lastly, it is an aid to concentration and to congregational participation. These are great gains. They make me thankful that the Church of England is a liturgical church.

Here, then, are four reasons why I believe in the Church of England. It is the historical church of the English. It has a sound biblical, theological basis. It is entrusted with a national mission. And it has in its liturgy a worthy vehicle for the praise of Almighty God through Jesus Christ in the power of the Holy Spirit.

Having made these positive statements, however, many evangelicals feel uncomfortable in the Church of England today. The Church of England which I have described is more of an ideal than a reality. Some would dismiss it as a 'paper' church, and not one of flesh and blood, bones and sinews. At the same time, from the second half of the twentieth century the evangelical movement has been growing in size, stature, maturity, scholarship and cohesion. It contains different strands (for example, reformed and charismatic), and is as much a coalition as a party. At the same time, there has been an assault on traditional Christian doctrine and morality. In consequence, the loyalty of ordinary church people has been severely strained. So what should we do?

THREE OPTIONS

The first option is *separation* or *secession* from the church. 'To stay in a doctrinally mixed church', some say, 'is an intolerable compromise. It gives the impression that we condone heresy. So, in order to maintain our evangelical testimony without compromise, we must get out.'

This is the position of independent evangelicals. Their overriding concern is to preserve the doctrinal purity of the church, which indeed is a right and proper concern. We should share their zeal for the truth, and their courage. But they tend to pursue the purity of the church at the expense of its unity, for which they seem to have no comparable concern. To be sure, there could be an extreme situation (for example, if the church were officially to repudiate the incarnation), when the only possible course would be to secede, since then the church would have ceased to be the church. We need to remember, however, that the sixteenth-century Reformers were themselves very reluctant schismatics. They did not want to leave the Catholic Church. On the contrary, they dreamed of a reformed Catholicism, a Catholic Church reformed according to Scripture, and were concerned for both its purity and its unity. Calvin wrote to Cranmer in 1552, for example, that the separation of churches was 'among the greatest misfortunes of our century'. The 'bleeding' state of the body of Christ affected him so deeply, he added, that he would 'not hesitate to cross ten seas' if he could help. 'Indeed, if learned men were to seek a solid and carefully devised agreement according to the rule of Scripture ... I think that for my part I ought not to spare any trouble or dangers.' That is (or should be) exactly the position of Anglican evangelicals today.

The second option that is before us is the opposite extreme. It is that of *compromise* and even *conformity*. This is the decision of some who say not only that they intend to stay in the Church of England at all costs, but that they would be willing to lose their distinctive evangelical witness.

I respect their desire to be responsible members of the Church of England, and (when it can be done with integrity) to minimize the differences between the traditions in the Church of England. But I think that their position is short-sighted. For we should have the courage, with humility, to bear witness to evangelical truth as we have been given to understand it. We claim no infallibility, and may be mistaken on certain points. We are open to have our minds changed if Scripture can be shown to require it. But we cannot conceal or smother our convictions. Our concern as evangelicals should certainly not be loyalty to a 'party'. Talk of a 'party' is a political concept. It conjures up toeing the party line, submitting to the party whip, and accepting the party discipline. Evangelical loyalty is not to a party, however, but to revealed truth, and in particular to the unique glory and adequacy of Jesus Christ.

The essence of the evangelical faith is that in Jesus Christ incarnate, crucified, raised and exalted, God has spoken and acted decisively and finally for the salvation of the world. In consequence, Jesus Christ is God's last word to the world; it is inconceivable that there should be any higher revelation than what he has given in his Son. Jesus Christ is also God's last deed for the salvation of the world; it is inconceivable that anything should need to be added to it. Nothing can be added either to what God has spoken in Christ or to what God has done in Christ. Both were *hapax*, 'once for all'. In Christ God's revelation and redemption are finished and complete.

That is why the hallmark of evangelicalism is an insistence on *sola scriptura* and *sola gratia*. They arise from *solus Christus*: Christ alone for revelation and redemption. Our concern, then, in maintaining a distinctive identity is not to be awkward or uncooperative or obstinate or partisan. It is to be faithful to the unique glory of the person and work of our Lord Jesus Christ. It is, we believe, for the good of the church and for the glory of God in Christ, that we should maintain our distinctive evangelical witness.

The third option is *comprehensiveness without compromise*, that is, staying in without caving in. Frankly it is the most painful of the three options. The other two options are easier because they are ways of cutting the Gordian knot. The first is to separate from everybody you disagree with, and so enjoy fellowship only with like-minded Christians. The second is to decline to maintain a distinctive testimony, and so regard all viewpoints as equally legitimate. These are opposite options (separation and compromise). But they have this in common: they are both ways of easing tension and escaping conflict. You either get out or you give in. The harder way, which involves walking a tightrope, is to stay in, while at the same time refusing to give in. This means living in a permanent state of tension, declining either to compromise or to secede.

Let me sum up. The way of separation is to pursue truth at the expense of unity. The way of compromise is to pursue unity at the expense of truth. The way of comprehension is to pursue truth and unity simultaneously, that is, to pursue the kind of unity commended by Christ and his apostles, namely unity in truth. Thus, Jesus prayed in John 17 for the truth, holiness, mission and unity of the church, while in Ephesians 4 Paul affirmed that there is 'one Lord, one faith, one baptism'. Unity and truth always walk hand in hand in the New Testament.

TWO KINDS OF COMPREHENSIVENESS

I have described the third option as 'comprehension'. I now have to qualify this. For what is often called the 'comprehensiveness' of the Church of England can be sought in one or other of two ways. On the one hand, there is an unlimited and unprincipled kind of comprehensiveness, from which no one is excluded. On the other hand, there is a limited and principled kind of comprehensiveness which lays down clear lines of demarcation.

The unlimited and unprincipled kind is a doctrinal free-for-all, in which no opinion is prohibited, let alone condemned as heretical. Rather, every viewpoint is welcomed as a contribution to, and even ingredient of, the resulting pot-pourri. It is this that Bishop J. C. Ryle dubbed 'a kind of Noah's ark', roomy enough to accommodate both the clean and the unclean.

The best lampoon of this view was developed by Ronald Knox in the marvellous piece which he entitled 'Reunion all Round' and included in his *Essays in Satire*.[2] It was sub-titled 'A plea for the inclusion within the Church of England of all Mahometans, Jews, Buddhists, Brahmins, Papists and Atheists'. In the new and universal church which he saw emerging, 'nobody will be expected to recite the whole Creed', he wrote, 'but only such clauses as he finds relish in; it being anticipated that, with good fortune, a large congregation will usually manage in this way to recite the whole Formula between them.'

Having dealt with differences between Christians, and differences between theists, he came finally to 'the Problem of Reunion with the Atheists'. In their case: 'We have only one single Quarrel to patch up, namely, as to whether God exists or not.' So he proposed to the theologians that, as we believe God to be both immanent and yet transcendent, we should be able to reconcile ourselves to 'the last final Antinomy, that God is both Existent and Non-existent'. He ended: 'Thank God, in these days of Enlightenment and Establishment, everyone has a right to his own Opinions, and chiefly to the Opinion, That nobody else has a right to theirs . . .'

This is not true ecumenism, however, but syncretism. Jesus our Lord and his apostles warned the church of false teachers. And I am glad that the Church of England has always officially recognized that unity must be in truth and that comprehensiveness must be principled, for this is the historic understanding of what true Anglican comprehensiveness is all about. The purpose of the Elizabethan settlement in the sixteenth century was to unite the nation within a national church committed to the supremacy of Scripture and to the Catholic creeds. As Dr Alec Vidler wrote,

> . . . the conception of Anglican comprehensiveness has been taken to mean that it is the glory of the Church of England to hold together in juxtaposition as many varieties of Christian faith and practice as are willing to agree to differ, so that the Church is regarded as a sort of league of religions . . . The principle of comprehension is that a church ought to hold the fundamentals of the faith, and at the same time allow for differences of opinion and interpretation in secondary matters, especially rites and ceremonies.[3]

It is a distinction which goes right back to the apostle Paul's insistence on loyalty to the apostolic faith, alongside liberty of conscience on secondary issues.

In conclusion, can we envisage a situation in which orthodox believers feel absolutely obliged to leave? Such an extreme situation might be:

- when an issue of first order is at stake, such as deserves the condemnation 'anti-Christ' (1 John 2:22) or 'anathema' (Galatians 1:8–9);
- when the offending issue is held not by an idiosyncratic minority of individuals but has become the official position of the majority;
- when the majority have silenced the faithful remnant, forbidding them to witness or protest any longer;
- when we have conscientiously explored every possible alternative;
- when, after a painful period of prayer and discussion, our conscience can bear the weight no longer.

Until that day comes, I for one intend to stay in and fight on.

So I do believe in the Church of England, in the rightness of belonging to it and of maintaining a faithful evangelical witness within it and to it. For I believe in the power of God's word and Spirit to reform and renew the church. I also believe in the patience of God. Max Warren wrote that 'the history of the Church is the story of the patience of God'.[4]

I HAVE A DREAM
OF A LIVING CHURCH

(24 November 1974)

In the Roman Catholic calendar, All Souls Day (2 November) commemorates the souls of the faithful departed who are regarded as being in purgatory. This being so, we at All Souls are often asked why such a committed evangelical church as ours should have been thus named. The answer is not far to find. We understand that the church founders were determined to build a church large enough to seat all the souls of the parish. Thus their resolve was not to commemorate all the souls of the dead, but rather to accommodate all the souls of the living.

The church was consecrated and opened to the public on 25 November 1824. So when the year 1974 dawned, we were anxious to mark the 150th anniversary of the dedication of the church. I was asked to preach on the nearest Sunday and to look into the future. With due apologies to Martin Luther King and his famous dream speech in Washington DC, I concluded my sermon with my own dream:

I have a dream of a church which is *a biblical church* —
   which is loyal in every particular to the revelation of
      God in Scripture,
   whose pastors expound Scripture with integrity and
      relevance, and so seek to present every member
      mature in Christ,
   whose people love the word of God, and adorn it
      with an obedient and Christ-like life,
   which is preserved from all unbiblical emphases,
      whose whole life manifests the health and beauty
      of biblical balance.
I have a dream of a *biblical* church.

I have a dream of a church which is *a worshipping
      church* —
   whose people come together to meet God and
      worship him,
   who know God is always in their midst and who
      bow down before him in great humility,
   who regularly frequent the table of the Lord Jesus,
      to celebrate his mighty act of redemption on the
      cross,
   who enrich the worship with their musical skills,
   who believe in prayer and lay hold of God in
      prayer,
   whose worship is expressed not in Sunday services
      and prayer gatherings only but also in their
      homes, their weekday work and the common
      things of life.
I have a dream of a *worshipping* church.

I have a dream of a church which is *a caring church* –
  whose congregation is drawn from many races,
    nations, ages and social backgrounds, and exhibits
    the unity and diversity of the family of God,
  whose fellowship is warm and welcoming, and never
    marred by anger, selfishness, jealousy or pride,
  whose members love one another with a pure heart
    fervently, forbearing one another, forgiving one
    another, and bearing one another's burdens,
  which offers friendship to the lonely, support to the
    weak, and acceptance to those who are despised
    and rejected by society,
  whose love spills over to the world outside, attractive,
    infectious, irresistible, the love of God himself.
I have a dream of a *caring* church.

I have a dream of a church which is *a serving church* –
  which has seen Christ as the Servant and has heard
    his call to be a servant too,
  which is delivered from self-interest, turned inside
    out, and giving itself selflessly to the service of
    others,
  whose members obey Christ's command to live in the
    world, to permeate secular society, to be the salt of
    the earth and the light of the world,
  whose people share the good news of Jesus simply,
    naturally and enthusiastically with their friends,
  which diligently serves its own parish, residents and
    workers, families and single people, nationals and
    immigrants, old folk and little children,

which is alert to the changing needs of society,
    sensitive and flexible enough to keep adapting its
    programme to serve more usefully,
which has a global vision and is constantly
    challenging its young people to give their lives in
    service, and constantly sending its people out to
    serve.
I have a dream of a *serving* church.

I have a dream of a church which is *an expectant
    church*—
whose members can never settle down in material
    affluence or comfort, because they remember that
    they are strangers and pilgrims on earth,
which is all the more faithful and active because it is
    waiting and looking for its Lord to return,
which keeps the flame of the Christian hope burning
    brightly in a dark, despairing world,
which on the day of Christ will not shrink from him
    in shame, but rise up joyfully to greet him.
I have a dream of an *expectant church*.

Such is my dream of a living church. May all of us share this
dream, and under God may the dream come true!

REFLECTIONS OF AN OCTOGENARIAN

(27 April 2001)

I celebrated my 80th birthday on 27 April 2001. One of the chief vices of the elderly is the tendency to reminisce. We seem to enjoy inflicting our memories on our hapless victims. Please therefore forgive me if in this appendix the personal pronoun is too prominent, and if I share with you just three convictions of this octogenarian.

The first is a conviction about *priorities*. I was appointed Rector of All Souls at the tender age of 29. I was much too young and inexperienced for such a heavy responsibility, and very soon everything got on top of me. The urgent regularly crowded out the important, and events would overtake me for which I was unprepared. I began to suffer the character-istic clerical nightmare: I was half way up the pulpit steps when I suddenly remembered that I had forgotten to prepare a sermon. I guess that at that time I was not far from a nervous breakdown.

Then one day in the early 1950s I attended a day-conference for clergy. One of the speakers was the Revd

L. F. E. Wilkinson, Principal of Oak Hill Theological
College. I remember nothing of his address except one
detail. He recommended every pastor to take a quiet day
once a month, to go right away from church and parish, to
allow God to draw him up into his heart and mind, to look
at things from the divine perspective, to focus on the
important and to adjust his priorities accordingly.

This commonsense advice came to me as a message from
God. It was exactly what I needed to be told, and I
immediately put it into practice. I returned home and went
through my engagement book for the rest of the year, and
wrote 'Q' for 'quiet' against one day every month.

Then, when my 'Q' day arrived, I would leave early for
the home of friends. They would put a room at my disposal,
bring me something to eat at meal times, and otherwise leave
me alone. Only my secretary knew where I was in case of an
emergency. I would get ten to twelve hours to myself.

I would keep for my monthly 'Q' day everything which
needed uninterrupted time – time to look ahead for the next
few weeks and months; time to see where I was going and
what had to be prepared; time to pray over some intractable
problem; time to reflect on the policy and programme of the
church; time to draft some difficult letters; time to sketch an
outline of a series of sermons; time to write an article; and
especially time to be quiet, to seek God's mind, and to
discern his perspective.

All I can say is that this little prudential arrangement
saved my life and my ministry. The burden of responsibility
was lifted. Although I was still challenged by the job, I was
not overwhelmed by it. In fact, so valuable did my monthly

'Q' day become that later, when I was exceptionally busy, I had a 'Q' day every fortnight, and even every week.

Secondly, let me share with you a conviction about *obedience*. John 14:21 is one of my favourite verses. Here are the words of Jesus: 'Whoever has my commandments and obeys them, he is the one who loves me. He who loves me will be loved by my Father, and I too will love him and show myself to him.'

This verse ends with a particularly precious promise: 'I will show myself to him (or her)', or 'I will manifest myself to him'. Is not this just what we are longing for, namely a clearer vision of Christ? Sometimes we do not sense his presence, and our vision is blurred. We may know the words of a rather old-fashioned prayer:

Lord Jesus, make yourself to me
A living bright reality;
More present to faith's vision keen
Than any outward object seen,
More dear, more intimately nigh
Than e'en the sweetest earthly tie.

But this promise of Jesus is conditional. He reveals himself only to his lovers. And who are his lovers? Not those who make loud protestations of love, and then go out like Peter to deny him. Not those who sing rather sentimental songs 'Jesus, I love you'. (It is all right, I sing them too, but they do not prove anything.) No, those who truly love the Lord Jesus are those who obey his commandments.

To sum up, the test of love is obedience, and the reward of love is a self-manifestation of Christ.

My third conviction concerns *humility*. No temptation is stronger or subtler than the insidious temptation to pride. Pastors and other church leaders are specially vulnerable, for we are always in the limelight. Our elevated pulpit is a dangerous place for any child of Adam to occupy. Our leadership easily degenerates into either autocracy or person-pleasing. We need constantly to remember that Jesus introduced into the world a new style of servant leadership:

> You know that those who are regarded as rulers of the Gentiles lord it over them, and their high officials exercise authority over them. Not so with you. Instead, whoever wants to become great among you must be your servant, and whoever wants to be first must be slave of all (Mark 10:42–44).

As the New Testament scholar T. W. Manson summed it up: 'In the Kingdom of God service is not a stepping-stone to nobility. It *is* nobility, the only nobility which is recognised.'

But how can this be? One thing I have learned is that humility is not a synonym for hypocrisy; it is, rather, another word for honesty. Humility is not pretending to be other than we are, but acknowledging the truth of what we are.

Michael Ramsey, an earlier Archbishop of Canterbury, spoke some wise and eloquent words about humility to a group of people on the eve of their ordination:

> (1) Thank God, often and always ... Thank God, carefully and wonderingly, for your continuing privileges ... Thankfulness is a soil in which pride does not easily grow.

(2) Take care about confession of your sins ... Be sure to criticize yourself in God's presence: that is your self-examination. And put yourself under the divine criticism: that is your confession ...

(3) Be ready to accept humiliations. They can hurt terribly, but they help you to be humble. There can be the trivial humiliations. Accept them. There can be the bigger humiliations ... All these can be so many chances to be a little nearer to our humble and crucified Lord.

(4) Do not worry about status ... There is only one status that our Lord bids us be concerned with, and that is the status of proximity to himself ...

(5) Use your sense of humour. Laugh about things, laugh at the absurdities of life, laugh about yourself, and about your own absurdity. We are all of us infinitesimally small and ludicrous creatures within God's universe. You have to be serious, but never be solemn, because if you are solemn about anything there is the risk of becoming solemn about yourself.[1]

In conclusion, it is at the cross of Christ that humility grows. As Emil Brunner wrote, other religions spare us the ultimate humiliation of being stripped naked and declared bankrupt before God. I have no greater desire than to make the apostle Paul's declaration authentically mine:

May I never boast except in the cross of our Lord Jesus Christ, through which the world has been crucified to me, and I to the world (Galatians 6:14).

NOTES

PREFACE

1. *What is the Spirit Saying...? A Report from the National Evangelical Anglican Celebration 1988*, pp. 8–9.
2. E.g. *Mission-Shaped Church*, is subtitled 'church planting and fresh expressions of church in a changing context' (Church House Publishing, 2004).
3. *Emerging Churches*, pp. 43–45.
4. *Mission-Shaped Church*, p. vii.
5. It was after I had completed this book that I came across Mark Dever's *Nine Marks of a Healthy Church* (Crossway, 2004). I am glad to note that his approach and mine are similar and supplement one another.

CHAPTER 1

1. *The Lambeth Conference 1958* (SPCK, 1958) part 2, p. 5.

CHAPTER 2

1. This report may be found in *Making Christ Known*, Historic Mission Documents from the Lausanne Movement 1974–1989 (Paternoster Press, 1996), pp. 57–72.
2. Malcolm Muggeridge, *Jesus Rediscovered* (Fontana Collins, 1969), p. 42.

CHAPTER 3

1. See *The Truth Shall Make You Free: The Lambeth Conference 1998* (Anglican Consultative Council, 1988), pp. 35, 43, 231.

2. I gladly refer my readers to Michael Green's mammoth book *Evangelism through the Local Church* (Hodder & Stoughton, 1990). Here are nearly 600 pages of guidance – theological, personal and practical – from one whose head, heart and hands are together committed to the evangelistic outreach of the local church.

3. *Essays in Liberality* (SCM, 19567), ch. 5.

4. Michael Ramsey, *Images Old and New* (SPCK, 1967), p. 14.

5. *The Church for Others* (WCC, 1967), pp. 7, 18–19.

6. Richard Wilke, *And Are We Yet Alive?* (Abingdon, 1986).

7. *Faith in the City* (Church House, 1985).

8. A. M. Hunter, *The Unity of the New Testament* (SCM, 1943), p. 7.

9. John Poulton, *A Today Sort of Evangelism* (Lutterworth, 1972), pp. 60–61, 79.

10. See, for example, Psalm 115:2.

11. For example, Psalm 115:4–7.

CHAPTER 4

1. See Ezekiel 3 and 33.

2. Richard Baxter, *The Reformed Pastor* (reprint Epworth Press, 1939), pp. 121–122.

CHAPTER 5

1. For instance, Romans 16:3–5; Philemon 1, 2.

2. Quoted in Leslie F. Church, *The Early Methodist People* (Epworth, 1948), p. 155.

3. Quoted by Church, *Ibid*, p. 153.

4. Quoted in J. S. Simon, *John Wesley and the Methodist Societies* (1923).

CHAPTER 6

1. S. C. Neill, *On the Ministry* (SCM, 1952), p. 74.
2. Donald Coggan, *Stewards of Grace* (Hodder, 1958), p. 46.
3. J. C. Ryle, *Principles for Churchmen* (4th ed. revised 1900), pp. 165–166.
4. Chad Walsh, *Campus Gods on Trial* (Macmillan, 1962), p. 95.
5. From his commentary on Deuteronomy 5:23ff.
6. C. H. Spurgeon, *An All-round Ministry* (1900, Banner, 1960), p. 236.
7. Phillips Brooks, *Lectures on Preaching* (1877, Baker 1969), pp. 159–160.
8. C. H. Spurgeon, *The Soulwinner* (Pilgrim Publications, 1978), p. 98.
9. D. M. Lloyd-Jones, *Preaching and Preachers* (Hodder, 1971), p. 97.

CHAPTER 7

1. The material of this chapter was first given as an exposition at 'The Gathering' in San Diego, California in 1998. It was subsequently preached in All Souls Church, Langham Place, London, and then published as a booklet both by Generous Giving in the USA, entitled *Stott on Stewardship*, and then in the UK by the International Fellowship of Evangelical Students and the Langham Partnership International, entitled *The Grace of Giving*.
2. *Making Christ Known* (Paternoster, 1996), p. 82.
3. See for example, Ephesians 3:1–9.

CHAPTER 8

1. K. S. Latourette, *A History of the Expansion of Christianity*, Vol. 7 (Eyre and Spottiswoode, 1945), p. 503.

2. From J. V. Taylor's review of *Calcutta* in his CMS Newsletter No. 360 (May 1972).
3. Martin Luther King, *Strength to Love* (Collins, 1963), p. 34.
4. Martin Luther King, *Stride Forward Freedom: The Montgomery Story* (Harper and Row, 1958), p. 198.
5. Robert Bellah in an interview in *Psychology Today*, January, 1976.
6. First published in 1870.

HISTORICAL APPENDIX I

1. I refer my readers specially to Timothy Dudley-Smith's careful account in *John Stott: A Global Ministry* (IVP, 2001), pp. 65–71.
2. Ronald Knox, *Essays in Satire* (Sheed & Ward, 1928).
3. Alec Vidler, *Essays in Liberality* (SCM, 1957).
4. Max Warren, *I Believe in the Great Commission* (Hodder & Stoughton, 1979).

HISTORICAL APPENDIX III

1. Michael Ramsey, 'Divine Humility', ch. 11 in *The Christian Priest Today* (1972, new rev. ed. 1988, SPCK), pp. 79–81.